I0132201

Teaching Social Skills
through Role Play

Teaching Social Skills through Role Play

Second Edition

Christopher Glenn

ROWMAN & LITTLEFIELD
Lanham • Boulder • New York • London

Published by Rowman & Littlefield
A wholly owned subsidiary of The Rowman & Littlefield Publishing Group, Inc.
4501 Forbes Boulevard, Suite 200, Lanham, Maryland 20706
www.rowman.com

Unit A, Whitacre Mews, 26–34 Stannary Street, London SE11 4AB

Copyright © 2017 by Christopher Glenn

All rights reserved. No part of this book may be reproduced in any form or by any electronic or mechanical means, including information storage and retrieval systems, without written permission from the publisher, except by a reviewer who may quote passages in a review.

British Library Cataloguing in Publication Information Available

Library of Congress Cataloging-in-Publication Data Is Available

ISBN 978-1-4758-3038-5 (cloth: alk. paper)
ISBN 978-1-4758-3039-2 (pbk: alk. paper)
ISBN 978-1-4758-3040-8 (electronic)

∞™ The paper used in this publication meets the minimum requirements of American National Standard for Information Sciences – Permanence of Paper for Printed Library Materials, ANSI/NISO Z39.48–1992.

Printed in the United States of America

This book is dedicated to the Franciscan Montessori Earth School in Portland, Oregon (http://fmes.org), and its cocreator, Mother Francine Cardew, who allowed me to conduct role play groups. It is also dedicated to the all the children who were in my role play groups, from 1984 to the present.

Contents

List of Role Plays

List of Creative Activities

List of Guided Imagery with Relaxation

Preface

Are you a *teacher* (Montessori or other) who wants to help your class bond and work together cohesively?

Are you a *parent* who would like to give your child a creative, self-motivating, hands-on, and interactive way of learning social skills with his or her friends?

Are you a *counselor or psychologist* with a children's group who wants to add a more active (and interactive) element?

Are you a *college student* learning how to work with children in an innovative, creative, and interactive manner?

Have you ever considered running an *after-school or weekend activity group* where the children go beyond just having fun and actually learn social and creative skills?

If you are one of these people, this book contains over 160 role plays, micro role plays, creative activities, and fantasy trips (guided imagery) for you. The activities can be used as-is, or they can be adjusted and altered using your common sense to better fit your needs.

While the target age range is eight to eleven years and older (third through sixth grades), in fact all of the activities in this book can include older children, among themselves, or even better, including children within the target age range. Younger children under age eight can learn vicariously by watching the activities and perhaps by taking a minor role.

Developed over a span of more than thirty years, this book contains descriptions of the best role plays and creative activities; the ones different groups of children love year after year. It also discusses what is important in setting up the role play group (both the atmosphere and specifics), particularly in terms of creating an environment conductive to social growth, self-understanding, and creativity.

The role plays and creative activities in this book, as well as the extensive notes on creating the atmosphere of the role play environment, encourage members toward cooperation, self-control, and the responsibility to run the group themselves. The focus is on the development of an open creative mind, self-control in an environment which the children create themselves, and personal emotional and social growth.

Role play can be used to encourage children to advance from one developmental stage to another. Members are encouraged to try on new roles in situations which foster self-understanding and social growth.

Role playing has become prevalent over the last several years, with one segment of the population using it for role play games such as World of Warcraft and Dungeons and Dragons and for other online multiplayer gaming. These fall under the category of fantasy gaming. This book is not about that. It is about *role playing as a psychological and educational interactive tool in teaching the skills and methods of self-understanding and social skills.*

There are many books available today for children activities. What is unique in this book is that most of the activities have significant self and social learning potential. While all the activities can be approached with a "let's just have fun!" attitude, the reader has the option to use the activities to teach social skills, self-control, self-understanding, and creativity to the children.

I started conducting role play groups for elementary aged children in 1984 at the Franciscan Montessori Earth School in Portland, Oregon. I was attracted to role playing as a means to assist emotionally healthy children grow both in self-understanding and in social skills, and I wanted the kids to develop a healthy sense of creativity as well.

As an undergraduate in an experimental college, I took three consecutive classes in Psychodrama.[1] On their website, the American Society of Group Psychotherapy and Psychodrama (asgpp.org) defines Psychodrama as:

Conceived and developed by Jacob L. Moreno, MD, psychodrama employs guided dramatic action to examine problems or issues raised by an individual (psychodrama) or a group (sociodrama). Using experiential methods, sociometry, role theory, and group dynamics, psychodrama facilitates insight, personal growth, and integration on cognitive, affective, and behavioral levels. It clarifies issues, increases physical and emotional well being, enhances learning and develops new skills.

By the time I graduated with a doctorate in psychology, I had spent a considerable time working with emotionally challenged children. With a desire to work with "everyday" children, I began to synthesize what I had learned in Psychodrama with skills and techniques applicable to working with emotionally healthy children, and role playing was born.

Already possessing a philosophy where I prefer to guide while letting the children take the lead, and working in a Montessori environment where this philosophy is important, I let the children teach me what worked and did not work. Original role play ideas came from the children, with me adjusting their ideas to include psychological and social content. I would also suggest ideas, and over the years, I developed and tweaked the ones the kids liked into what you see in this book.

Finding that ninety minutes was a long time for just role playing, I began to add additional content such as creative activities (usually with a psychological element), micro role plays (role plays that take one to five minutes and use one to three children), and guided imagery (here called fantasy trips, something to which the kids can better relate).

As you use the role plays and creative activities in this book, you will be guided by accompanying notes which consider classroom variations, some typical problems for which to watch, as well as the underlying psychological meaning of the activity.

Because I utilized my psychology roots while creating the role plays (as well as in selecting the creative activities), the material is ready to use (and to be adapted to your personal needs) for psychologists and others trained to advanced levels.

A hidden benefit is that many of the activities described herein can be used among adults. Some of the role plays and creative activities can be adapted for use in a variety of situations including staff retreats, friend get-togethers, family reunions, and even parties.

NOTE

1. Moreno, J. L. *Psychodrama*. (New York: Beacon House, 1969).

Introduction

While this book primarily is meant for teachers, parents, counselors, psychologists, and lay people who work with children, the *casual reader* will find, after the chapter 5 introduction, role plays and creative activities which can be used in almost any setting from children and adult parties to casual weekend or summer fun, without reading other parts of the book. The first four chapters focus on procedures to create an activity group which will meet over several weeks, months, or an entire school year.

Teachers can make excellent use of several role plays and creative activities during the first week of school. Discussed in chapter 1 (Classroom Role Plays) will be specific role plays and creative activities which can be used to help build class bonding, identity, and interpersonal comfort. Also considered is the use of in-class role plays during the school year. Material in this book was created in a Montessori environment but is written in common terms for all teachers.

This book can be considered an *experiential curriculum* in teaching self-understanding and social skills, both general interaction and mediation.

Parents can make use of role plays and creative activities on the weekends and holiday breaks, including summer. The book is written in language that can be read and understood by many ten-year-olds, so choice of what to do from the book can become a parent-child interaction experience. The activities can be done with kids on their own, or with adults, if the child desires.

Counselors and psychologists can jump right in and choose role plays addressing target issues.

College students and *those running after-school activity groups* can rely on chapters 2–4 for details in setting up the group environment and running the group, as well as specific procedures for the first three group meetings.

DEFINITION OF ROLE PLAY

Role playing is experiential play-acting where the scenario contains some psychological and/or social theme through which personal and social understanding and/or growth can occur. However, sometimes, with children, role play is Just For Fun and may not address any psychosocial themes beyond those encompassed by all role plays (see "psychosocial considerations" in chapter 5).

It is effective to describe role play by use of examples:

• Adventures in Aftercare: Two children playing child care workers step out of the room while other members create scenarios of what can go wrong (she won't share her markers, he kicked me under the table). The players step back into the room with the scenario underway and must deal with what is presented to them.
• Self-Empowerment: Parents forget how to take care of themselves; children must help and teach parents.
• Robot science experiment: Create a robot, teach it to have feelings, and interact with others.
• Aliens!: Peaceful first contact; aliens land in a forest with children playing. How do you communicate?
• Campout disasters: Natural disasters occur or perhaps the adults disappear. What do you do?

In addition to role plays, there are three other methods of participation considered in this book. Micro role plays (chapter 6) are short-duration scenarios that can enhance a creative response and can serve as filler for a role play that runs short. They can be used in the classroom to facilitate a feeling of comfort in expression. Creative activities (chapter 7) are useful at the end of the group as a closing game or to fill time for a scheduled group, and also at the beginning of the group (and in the classroom) to loosen members up or to help calm and focus them if they are somewhat wild. Fantasy trips (guided imagery) are considered in chapter 8. Akin to role plays of the mind, the group leader reads to the players a story which involves them and has specific psychological content.

If you have never run an activity group, this book begins with detailed notes on how to prepare the role play environment, its physical layout, and psychological atmosphere. You don't need to have psychological training (although if you do, you can bring your skills into the mix), but it helps if you have some familiarity in working with groups of children.

Role plays and creative activities have been categorized on a simple-to-complex continuum. While there is much overlap, this method can guide the user in choice of activity. Simple role plays and creative activities are used earlier in the year, with complexity increasing with the skill level of the group.

A key feature of this book is that after each role play and creative activity is described, each one lists variations (the majority have classroom variations), the psychology behind the activity, cautions, and additional notes, and each concludes with a subheading for "your notes," where you can record your reactions and comments as you use the material.

Chapter 1

Classroom Role Plays and Creative Activities

The activities described in this book, as a group, can be considered an *experiential curriculum*. Unlike academic subjects where curricula are usually step-by-step with regular verification of learning, when teaching social skills to elementary-aged children, it becomes more of, "here is a set of skills to be learned throughout the school year." Instead of a rigid order, what is taught on any given day depends on teacher, classroom, and individual student needs, as well as the level of student self-control on that day. Some role plays and creative activities take more self-control than others.

The role plays and creative activities in this book that include classroom variations have been written for use during the school year, as need arises. In this chapter, we take the most appropriate role plays and creative activities to use in the orientation period or the first week of school, adding comments specific to this time period.

THE FIRST WEEK OF SCHOOL

The first week of school, when many students in your classroom don't truly know each other (i.e., their personalities), provides a rich opportunity to use role plays and creative activities to help bond the class. In a (three grades in one classroom) Montessori environment, about a third of students are new to the classroom, but in most environments, the majority of students are new. The first order of the day is to get the children to become one cohesive classroom, where the usual cliques are discouraged, while meeting new people is encouraged. The cliques may still form, but less strongly when everyone has had "emotional" contact with everyone else. Class discussion of the effects of forming into closed cliques can be the motivator, the springboard creating the desire to conduct some on-target role playing and creative activities. Discussion of how "open" the cliques will be might be productive as well.

First-of-year classroom role plays and creative activities should include most or all of the class participating, individually or in subgroups. However, allowing the occasional student to watch is considered a valid vicarious learning experience and can be justified on an individual basis, although these students should be expected to contribute in the ensuing group discussion. In chapter 5, the Role Play chapter, later in this book, the "classroom variations" focus on use of the role play later in the school year. In this classroom-focused chapter, the description is copied from the Role Plays chapter and is followed by comments specific to first of year classroom role plays.

Four Role Plays

Stranded on an Island

In this role play, students divide up (or are divided up) into a few task-oriented subgroups.

> Be it tropical, desert, arctic, or wherever, the players get to the island via some calamity (e.g., shipwreck, plane crash) which is also enacted. The goal is to get the kids to focus on survival, that is, cooperation, gathering food, making shelter, and finding a way home. The addition of a native tribe is common, at which time some players switch roles to be the natives.

Classroom: Assign and/or choose roles while students are still in their chairs, then set up the environment (move chairs and desks, specify where the water and land are, briefly describe what the island looks like right in front of them). The subgroups should form around tasks such as find food and water, make shelters, secure camp for safety, cook food, make *defensive* (defensive only) weapons, maybe plan evening entertainment, and/or campfire discussion topics (a role play within a role play). The teacher should be active in the choice of roles. Use your initial sense of personality and potential bad pairings, or of choice of role being too difficult to use self-control (e.g., the hyper kid might have difficulty being a hunter, the shy kid should be encouraged toward more active roles). Roles can be switched by the teacher at any time. You might need to switch a leader into a role that makes the role play move forward, or ask the low self-control kid to sit and watch for a few minutes. You should notice, point out, and ask to make corrections to things that could not happen, such as finding a working airplane, a restaurant, a time machine, or launching a satellite to reestablish cell service. Make it as real as possible. Unlike during-the-year role plays, your primary goal is to get kids to interact with other kids with whom they don't ordinarily interact. So you might pair up two very unlikely people, and you also might want to increase the number of bi-gender subgroups. Feel free to pause the role play to discuss what is happening and to remind the students of the goal, to get unlikely people to interact, to get to know each other's personalities. The use of pause in the classroom (where a shout may not be appropriate) is best done with a bell, a preplanned clapping sequence, or some other easily distinguishable noise. Role plays rarely finish. At some point, it becomes clear that the role play has run its course, and not much new is going on. You could even ask the class if there is anything else we might get from this role play, or is it time for the group discussion.

The discussion must be respectful, *allowing absolutely no put downs*, none at all. Remind them insults push people away and close them emotionally, which is the opposite of what we are doing. Focus the discussion on what worked and did not work in terms of cooperation, mediation organizing in general, and getting tasks done, and the flip side; feelings of not being included. Consider the effects of different leader styles, or no leader at all. In discussion, try not to mention specific people by name.

What Am I Feeling?

Split into two groups. Give a different emotion to each group, and give them time to make up skits which portray each emotion. Then each group takes a turn displaying their emotion, while the other group tries to guess what the emotion is. After the first few, have the groups choose the emotions themselves. Usually create a semicircle of chairs for the audience. Discuss other ways you could have portrayed that emotion.

Classroom: Begin by discussing emotions in general. Ask students to name all emotions, and write these on the board as they are stated. Divide the class into groups of six or eight students each. Then, within each of these large subgroups, either you or the group further divides their members into two equal small subgroups. You go up to each of the pairs of small subgroups and give each a different emotion. Since the large subgroups will not be interacting with each other, you could give the same pair of emotions to each large subgroup (without telling them), so that you have the option of large subgroups watching the skits of each other.

Group discussion can focus on ease and difficulty of expressing a feeling (and how ease and difficulty vary by emotion), how it felt if the emotion was not guessed. Discuss why it's important to express many emotions both in facial expression and in body posture, and discuss when it is important or OK to hide a feeling.

How to Be a Dummy (and Ventriloquist)

Form into pairs and have each pair decide who will first be the dummy. Give someone two dummies if you have an odd number of players. The ventriloquist stands just behind and slightly to the side of the dummy and places his or her hand on the dummy's back or shoulder. It is important to physically touch your dummy because it increases the sense of the dummy having no will.

Classroom: Follow as described in the Role Plays chapter. Before your students form into pairs, talk with them about the reason for this whole thing, to get to know others in the class. Then ask them to choose partners who they don't know or know the least. Be proactive in any pairings; you may have an idea about a few pairings, and you may want to break up some pairs, for instance, two hyperactive students. You may want to make girl-boy pairs. The class discussion afterward should focus on the issues described under the Psychology subheading in the Role Play chapter.

The Same Message

This role play is similar to What Am I Feeling but instead focuses on ideas instead of just one emotion.

Divide the group in half. Choose one message, with some psychological content if possible. Each group has about five minutes to create a skit to act out the message. After both groups perform their skits, everyone discusses how and why each message was different. After a while, have the players make up messages.

Classroom: In the classroom environment with more people, divide the class into groups of five or six individuals, and give them ten minutes to make up their skit. You may want to do the dividing. Your goal is to have a mix of leaders and followers, of less and more serious students and of genders. You can choose the topic or, even better, specify some guidelines and have the students choose the topic. Guidelines are simple: the topic must be relevant to your classroom, have a psychological or feeing focus, involve differences of opinion, and as always, be done respectfully.

In discussion, mention that there are two goals for this role play. The first is to see how one topic can be addressed so differently, and that can be discussed. But the more important goal in this first week of school role play is to identify and discuss various strategies and personalities used, and how that affected others and the group as a whole. Who asserted themselves as leaders? Did they ignore or include the more quiet people? Were they more interested in their own ideas at the expense of others' ideas? Did the less serious students delay or side track the process? Were the more serious students able to help? Did anyone's interaction style change as the group progressed?

Five Creative Activities

Mirror

> Pair up members, with a threesome if you have an odd number of participants. First, each pair chooses a leader, then the leader makes slow and controlled movements, including facial gestures, while the other member follows. Switch roles and redo.

Classroom: Use as is. The younger students will find this more interesting than the older ones, so if you see boredom, suggest more complicated movements and facial expressions. This one goes quickly, so it is best to add another creative activity. You may want to use this activity first, as an icebreaker.

Discussion can be brief and focus on what it *felt* like to lead or follow. Discuss how those feelings apply in the classroom.

Who Laughs First?

> Everyone stands or sits in a circle and looks into each other's eyes. The person who laughs first can either take a step backward out of the circle until just one is left, or just redo with everyone. After each round, discuss what one can do with feeling and thought (but not with muscles) to suppress the laugh. Repeat to test new strategies.

Classroom: Start off with smaller groups, about five or six each, then combine groups until the entire class does this. The students should look directly into the eyes of others, use only blank faces, and use no expressions or "scrunching" the face together to suppress a laugh. Consider any sort of smile a laugh, including the attempt to hold it in (i.e., compressing lips). When someone laughs, they take a step backward out of the circle, until just one is left. It is actually possible to have two finalists who continue not to laugh, in which case you could up the stakes by allowing facial expressions, or you could call both winners. Also, you could have a final round consisting of the subgroup winners.

Before you start and when you see it happen, discuss playing fair. Make sure people don't use tricks to not see, such as crossing the eyes, not looking directly into others' eyes, fast blinking, and similar avoidance methods. Discuss how that is not fair to the group, or that it disrespects the group.

Discussion can include feelings of discomfort when looking into another's eyes, what type of self-control does it take to do this, and whether learning self-control here can carry over to other classroom behaviors.

Circle Story

Sit on chairs in a circle. One person begins a story with about one to three sentences, leaving off in the middle of a sentence, then the next person continues the story, and this continues around the circle as many times as you want. Usually, you start the first few stories until members catch on. For example, "On a warm summer day, I was sitting in the middle of a lake in a row boat, when suddenly. . . . "

Classroom: It is best that the teacher start the story, but it is important to *not* focus on current needs or on a first week of school topic. This is to prevent the story from possibly turning negative. With the goal of class bonding, a fantasy would be best. For example, "I was walking in the forest (or desert) when I saw, just standing there, a door. Since it said in big red letters 'Do Not Open,' I opened the door, and. . ."

Be sure to keep this moving quickly. You could participate too. When passed to the next person, that person can say "skip" if nothing comes to mind, or you could set up beforehand that if there was a pause of more than two seconds, the following person would just pick it up and continue.

Discussion can focus on how hard it is to have an idea of what to say when it's not your turn and not being able to say it (i.e., using self-control), the frustration of having to suddenly drop what you planned to add because the person before you threw you a curve, and on what happened if someone added something off topic.

Hands in the Middle

Members stand in a tight circle with shoulders touching. They reach in with their arms and hands, and each hand grabs one other hand. The group then tries to untangle themselves into one large circle without letting go of each other. Some will end up facing into the circle, while others will end with facing out. Tell members to loosely hold the other hand, to let the hand rotate as you move about.

Classroom: This is an activity of which you or some students may have heard under a variety of different names. Start off with subgroups of five or six students. Combine subgroups and redo. Emphasize moving slowly for safety. Discuss the need to communicate within the subgroups, to not just move on your own. Ask the class if they want to try the whole class, emphasizing the need to be careful. Often someone will have a momentary pain of a twisted wrist, but there should be no injury if people are careful and respectful and allow hands and wrists to rotate when holding. There can be quite a sense of accomplishment if the whole class can do it.

Discussion can focus on whether a leader stepped forward (or if s/he was chosen), perhaps how it went without a leader, did you feel like a pawn or did you feel you contributed to the process, as well as the general sense of camaraderie the activity created.

How Long Is a Minute?

Have the members sit so they can't see a clock. Using a watch with a second indicator, or using a "count up" stopwatch so it does not sound a tone when time is up, first set a time frame for the members. Begin with twenty seconds. Say "ready, set, go," then time your twenty seconds. When each member thinks it's time, they quietly raise their hand until all have done so. Then try thirty seconds.

Classroom: Use this as is. It is an excellent opening or closing activity because it naturally calms people down. As the time progresses, you try to note how early or late students raise their hands, in order to give them feedback for the next round. This can be difficult, trying to watch the time while hands are going up, but with practice and peripheral vision, it can be done. After the first few times, ask the class how many seconds they want to time. Try to point out the number of seconds the first raised hand was early, point to one or more students who were accurate within a second or two, and note how many seconds late the last person was. If the students look around *after they raise their hands*, they can judge where they fell, based on a few examples.

Discussion may not be necessary, but it might be interesting to ask the class what about this activity made them calm down (or not).

DURING THE SCHOOL YEAR

When it comes to the activities described in this book, the needs of teachers are somewhat different from those of parents or leaders of an activity group. Role plays in the classroom tend to be more organized and formal as compared to after-school or home-based role plays. With a full class of children, several may not get to participate (although they learn a lot vicariously by projecting themselves into the role play). Usually, in the classroom, a specific topic is chosen beforehand based on classroom need (e.g., there is a problem of kids excluding less popular kids), the teacher mostly assigns the roles, and the role play itself is kept on a more narrow track, maintaining focus on the chosen topic.

Over the years, role playing in the classroom has been used in many settings with many types of children and target situations. Here are a few examples. Role playing has been used in kindergarten and first-grade classes to increase overall participation and to help the students to become better advocates for themselves,[1] and also to improve social skills.[2] It has been used in fourth-grade classes to teach students to effectively handle bullying situations[3] and in an English as a Second Language class (in England) to help learn language.[4] It has been used to help students from kindergarten through fourth grade to understand what animals need to survive.[5] Role playing has been used in fifth-grade sports to increase sportsmanship in physical education classes.[6] It has been used in middle school to make student learning more participatory, stimulating, and imaginative.[7]

In a more general sense, an excellent and practical "how-to" source is *Role-Playing Methods in the Classroom*,[8] and many suggestions discussed in this chapter came from chapter 3 of that book. Full text is available online for free through ERIC (ED075276).

Many of the role plays and creative activities in this book can be adapted and used in a classroom environment. Among the fifty role plays discussed in chapter 5, thirty-one of them have a subsection for Classroom Variations, as do twenty-one of the twenty-seven creative activities.

The best way for a teacher to approach these ways to teach social skills and self-understanding is to think of them as suggestions to guide in developing his or her own topic-specific role plays. For example, the role play of Adults Forget How to Take Care of Themselves may suggest a scenario where a student forgets to bring in his or her report assignment, or as suggested under Variations, the teacher forgets how to teach. Micro role plays can be used initially to facilitate a feeling of comfort when expressing emotions, and the guided imagery stories can be used as a more interactive method instead of just reading a story.

It is vital that everyone, teacher and students alike, learn to feel comfortable with each other. Some children need to be given permission to act out negative behaviors within the role play, and this becomes more effective as everyone begins to feel comfortable in expressing emotions. It is good to have an ability to laugh at yourself. In the variation discussed earlier where the teacher forgets how to teach, the teacher would need to feel comfortable in allowing a student to play him or her, and the student playing the teacher would need to feel comfortable enough with the teacher so as to play the role with real feelings.

The first classroom role plays should be simple and direct. In fact, the goal of the first role play could be to achieve some degree of comfort in expressing feelings in the group. Teacher comfort comes first—if the teacher feels comfortable, the students are more likely to feel the same.

A good way for the teacher to achieve this is to approach the role play as a collaborative effort. Involve the students in the process. For example, after describing the role play, ask the students to identify what roles are needed. Afterward, ask the students for feedback and suggestions ("should we do this role play again with different people or move on?"), and feel comfortable admitting nonsuccess ("well, that one didn't come out as I thought it would. What can we do differently next time?").

Usually, classroom role plays begin with a discussion of guidelines. Primarily, everyone needs to feel comfortable in being able to express opinions and emotions. Respect can be considered an overall value. Play the teacher *with respect*, play the "problem" student *respectfully*. Nonetheless, feelings can be hurt, and people should feel comfortable in saying so. After the role play, it is important to hold a debriefing discussion where everyone, including those who only watched the role play, can share similar feelings and experiences.

The actual role play usually begins with a warm-up exercise or game. The micro role plays discussed in chapter 6 can be used for warm up; in fact, they can be targeted toward individual students' proclivities, interests, and personalities. Another method to "loosen up" the students is to have them, for example, pretend they are walking through very deep snow or on marbles. Perhaps divide the class into subgroups and have them pretend to toss back and forth a porcupine or hot potato.

After the warm up, the teacher presents the actual role play topic, something s/he has decided the class needs to learn such as accepting others who are being excluded from a group, issues related to sharing of materials, letting another join in an ongoing game, and mediation issues. In order to allow for greater participation, the teacher can have players switch roles with students who are watching as the role play progresses.

Here are a few brief examples.

- Can I play too? Four students are playing a game outside on a blanket and a fifth wants to join. Do it several ways, such as two say no and two say yes or all four ignore the newcomer. At each stage, discuss feelings and strategies used by the newcomer.
- Switch this one around where three or four students see a new student standing apart and ask him or her to join in a task or game. Have the new student react in different ways and discuss how each felt and what worked or did not work.
- Some students are working on a project where lots of papers are scattered about on a table or an area on the floor, and a student rushes by and accidentally disturbs the papers. Practice some typical reactions to this scenario and discuss best strategies.
- Two students are arguing over who goes first. Try different methods and discuss.

A more generalized example is to hold a class discussion using seven or eight students. Provide some topic examples from which the students can choose, for example, we have $100 to spend on X and what do we do, we're planning a field trip and want the class to choose the beach, mountains, or desert. In this scenario, you could assign personalities such as the noncompromiser, the bossy leader, the interrupter, the person who agrees with everyone, the nay-sayer, and the jokester who takes the focus off the group process and onto himself or herself.

Finally, while it is very important to hold a class discussion after the role playing, it is equally important to reinforce what was taught in the coming days. When you see something happening which parallels the role play, remind the class about what they did in role play, what strategies worked and didn't work.

The length of the role play is an important consideration. Fifty years ago, Chesler and Fox suggested fifteen minutes for grades one to three, thirty minutes for grades four to six, and older students could handle forty minutes.[9] With today's children, these numbers may be low. This writer has run several upper elementary (grades four to six combined) groups for over an hour. How much time you have may be the primary determinant of role play length.

Controversial issues deserve some mention. It is important that class participants do not feel singled out. The teacher might present a more generalized role play topic such as, how do you deal with a student joining the class mid-term? This would be analogous to dealing with the left-out student. Also, the student(s) with the target problem would not be asked to play that role in the role play (but they could volunteer).

It is important to provide a positive experience, to show successful ways to resolve the situation. Perhaps first act out a problem, then act out (i.e., model) positive resolutions. This will help the class to bond and will encourage them toward using positive behaviors.

In the coming chapters, teachers can apply some of the broader concepts to the classroom. For example, in the next chapter, where the preparation of the role play environment is discussed, the teacher can create a space that is not too large or small in which to conduct the role play by having students move their desks to create said space, and s/he can tailor the teacher role to encourage student ownership of the process. The major take-aways from chapter 3 which considers the first group meeting could be that a student always has the right to not participate but to watch vicariously and the need to show respect and to use self-control. Chapter 4 suggests that, as the class becomes more familiar with the role play process, they take more and more control of the process.

NOTES

    1. Boyd, S. L., Lillig, K. A., and Lyon, M. R. "Increasing Student Participation and Advocacy of Primary Students through Role Play, Teacher Modeling, and Direct Instruction of Communication Skills" (Masters dissertation, Saint Xavier University, 2007). ERIC Number: ED498927.

2. Brodeski, J. and Hembrough, M. "Improving Social Skills in Young Children" (Masters dissertation, Saint Xavier University, 2007). ERIC Number: ED496699.

3. Anderson, S. and Swiatowy, C. "Bullying Prevention in the Elementary Classroom Using Social Skills" (Masters dissertation, Saint Xavier University, 2008). ERIC Number: ED503060.

4. Grant, K. and Mistry, M. T. "How Does the Use of Role-Play Affect the Learning of Year 4 Children in a Predominately EAL Class?," *Education 3–13*, 38, No. 2, (2010): 155–164.

5. Worch, E. A., Scheuermann, A. M., and Haney, J. J. "Role-Play in the Science Classroom," *Science and Children*, 47, No. 1, (2009): 54–59.

6. Shulman, M. D. "Increasing Positive Sportsmanship in Elementary Physical Education Using Prosocial Behavior Interventions" (Masters dissertation, Saint Xavier University, 2013). ERIC Number: ED541339.

7. Wilson, A. "Using Role Play in Middle-School and Secondary Classes," *Educational Perspectives*, 39, No. 2, (2006): 23–26.

8. Chesler, M. and Robert Fox. *Role-Playing Methods in the Classroom*. Chicago: Science Research Associates, Inc., 1966.

9. Chesler and Fox. *Role-Playing Methods in the Classroom*. 19.

Chapter 2

The Preparation of the Role Play Environment

The actual physical environment is loaded with psychological meaning, making it difficult to separate the two.

THE PSYCHOLOGY OF THE PHYSICAL ENVIRONMENT

For elementary aged children, it is best to use a room that is large enough for the role players to move around and create various imaginative environments, but small enough to encourage the entire group to work together. A large room becomes more difficult for two reasons. First, it encourages a loss of self-control. Second, it is natural for the group to split into subgroups, recombine, and split into different subgroups as the role play progresses. But in a large room, it becomes more difficult for these subgroups to be aware of what each other is doing, and this, in turn, makes it more difficult for the subgroups to recombine into either one large group or different subgroups as the role play progresses.

Most kids in the target age range prefer to sit on chairs rather than gathering on the floor, and feedback made clear that they thought chairs to be the mature choice. While carpeting is not absolutely necessary, it is good for role play, if only because it seems less like a classroom. Also, players make extensive use of the third dimension, spending considerable time on the floor, and for that, carpeting or a rug is nice.

Usually, the role play group is held in someone else's room (or a common room used by many). One of the first things to be done is to set up the environment, and this is where the members start to understand what it is to run their own group (with the adult as more of a guide), work together, and plan beforehand. An open space is needed, and assuming a layout of chairs and desks or tables, the first things to decide are where the open space will be and where to move which desks or tables out of the way. Regardless of desk or table size, it is a good idea to require at least two people to move any piece of furniture (except chairs) in order to get the group to begin working together. For tables large enough for all members to fit around, ask that *all* members move it; a strong lesson in communication, cooperation, and self-control. Be patient; rarely does this go smoothly the first time.

Require that furniture be used in the way for which it was intended. Chairs are for sitting (with feet on the floor), and tables are not for sitting or lying on, unless it's something like a hospital scene where a table or two/three desks can serve as a bed. This supports the efforts toward self-control.

PSYCHOLOGICAL CONSIDERATIONS

This section considers the group leader's role, including knowledge and experience with psychology in children, recruiting, self-control, length and size of group, to snack or not, playing animals, group discussions, and the group hug.

The Group Leader's Role

Although this interpretation of role play is primarily psychological, it is direct and simple in approach. Adults who value psychological understanding can do a lot to help children understand themselves in role play and can use common sense in running a role play group. Those with master level or higher counseling skills and experience can bring that valuable knowledge to the group. Less experienced or knowledgeable people can approach the group with the idea of "just having fun" and not going beyond that.

In fact, doing psychological therapy in role play is not appropriate in the classroom or in an after-school activity group. If the reader has graduate level training and experience, draw the line at interpretation. It is appropriate to provide feedback to expressed feelings and demonstrated behaviors. It is not appropriate to offer interpretations of such feelings and behaviors. For example, every week a child wants to play a little kid. After two or three meetings, the group leader might draw the child aside and mention to her that she tends to choose to play only young children. That is feedback. What would be left unsaid is to offer further words about why this behavior might be. It may be okay to ask the child why s/he makes that choice and responds in terms of what s/he says (often which is "I don't know"). Key is to encourage her to think about why she makes that choice, and this actually is a gentle way to suggest to her that she try other roles.

Role play deals with real feelings. When the group leader say this to the kids, mention that in the classroom you learn about biology, math, and history, but in role play, you learn about feelings. Dealing with real feelings in the 8–11+ age range means that sometimes feelings get hurt, and it also means one might be afraid or embarrassed to open up for fear of being teased. Fortunately, with the emotionally healthy, forgiveness is usually quick, especially after the group has bonded. With a zero tolerance for put-downs and insults, and with several mentions that members of the group should learn to help each other out, including away from the group such as on the playground, this sharing of feelings can be a particularly bonding experience.

Bring up the concept of confidentiality, although not calling it that. First ask how they would feel if they overheard someone talking about them. Then, suggest that what happens in the role play group should only be discussed with other children in a general sense and not to mention specific names when doing so. The exception is to encourage them to talk about role play with their parents. However, in this age range, it is common that the child does not spontaneously share details with the parent about role play.

If the group as a whole comes that day with some degree of self-control, the leader can sit back and just guide the process as needed. Other days, however, require a slightly more authoritarian approach because the kids have difficulty focusing. As much as possible, let them make choices about what to do. In chapter 5 which considers how the group chooses a role play, this value of "kids in charge" will become quite evident.

Sometimes the group leader can participate in the role play. Usually, this is when the kids ask the leader to play a particular role or when there are several absent members. However, being able to step back and watch the entire scene can help the leader to make good choices in assisting the role play toward its psychosocial goals, and it can be difficult to do this and play a role as well.

Instead of participating, those with masters or doctoral level training can best help the kids understand themselves when one can observe and drop in a comment (feedback) to one or more players. Also, it is easier to move from subgroup to subgroup, understand what is happening, and make suggestions to either bring the groups together in a common task or to suggest an overall enhancement or change to the role play (e.g., if it is not working well). Those with no psychological training might more easily be participants.

Sometimes a parent or staff member has asked if they could observe the role play group. In an ideal world, being observed would be up to the group to decide, and usually most members this age will say no. When asked why, they say they don't want adults to watch them. However, if it is an adult with whom the kids feel comfortable, that may make the observation okay.

This attitude reveals some of the benefit of role play where inhibition is not a good thing (unless it is part of a role, such as playing a shy person). Maybe the kids don't realize it, but they are working out "growing up" issues from their subconscious, making direct observation uncomfortable.

Allowing the group members to make this choice was more acceptable in the past. In today's world, it may be necessary to allow any parent or appropriate school staff member to observe. But in order to help the group members feel comfortable with the visitor, the observer should be required to sit in on the opening group discussion where you may chat for a few minutes, then settle down to make up a role play. At that time, the observer would have the choice to observe or participate. Further, the guest observer or participant should be encouraged to participate in any ending discussion. Be sure to mention confidentiality, that visitors should not discuss role play in ways where individuals could be identified.

Recruiting

While recruiting members happens before the group starts, the role of the group leader needed to be discussed first, because modeling this role happens in the recruiting.

Appendix A contains an information and sign-up sheet to be distributed to parents and should be significantly edited to meet your situation. A Word copy of this and the other appendices is available for download and editing from the publisher (see appendices for link). This current version has been tweaked over several years to emphasize the needs for self-control, trying new things, and maintaining a positive attitude.

Many parents do not read the hand-out. While a shorter version might be more readable, the psychological emphasis of the group calls for a more complete written explanation.

In consideration of members participating in the group, informed consent becomes important. This sign-up sheet includes a section where the child must sign his or her name as well, after discussing role play with the parent. Since it is uncommon to ask for signature in this age range, doing so reinforces both the uniqueness of this after-school activity group and the child focus of the group.

On the day that the handouts are distributed, with permission of the teachers and on a class-by-class basis, take the eligible students (e.g., third graders) into the hall (or an open nearby room if available) and describe role play to them. It is important for the children to meet the group leader and feel comfortable with him or her. Be sure to show them the information and sign-up sheet. The important part is to emphasize several times that an interested child must mention role play to his or her parent, including pointing out the sign-up sheet. The motivation to join comes from the child, and this is particularly appropriate because the kids run the group themselves (as much as their self-control allows at any one moment).

In this fifteen-minute discussion, begin by describing what is role play, primarily through the use of examples.

> Role play is a safe place where you get to make up stuff and act it out. For example, one of the favorite role plays is called *Aliens*. The group splits into half, with half being human kids playing in a forest and the other half are aliens who land their space ship nearby. You get to do it twice so everyone can play a human and an alien. They come out of their spaceship, and you have to figure out how to make peaceful first contact. But remember, the aliens don't speak human. In fact, they are so different that simple gestures such as shaking their hand might mean something different. If you were the alien and a human put out his or her hand, in alien that might mean the human is offering his or her hand for dinner! Or maybe marriage! So how do you communicate with people with different language and where movements or gestures might mean something very, very different?
>
> Or maybe you go on a campout with your family and your friend's family, and when you wake up, the adults have disappeared. Can you figure out what happened to them *and* how to survive on your own?
>
> Or maybe you get shipwrecked on a desert island or stranded on the space station.

At this point, often some kids suggest role play ideas themselves, which is kind of fun to hear. Usually, by now some kids are having self-control issues. Without mentioning or looking at the offenders, discuss the importance of self-control in the groups, mentioning that a wild child would not be a good match for role play and would not be happy. Ask the kids for examples of loss of self-control, but require them to not mention any names (although often most of the kids know who is being described). Emphasize the need for self-control several times throughout this discussion. Often kids are good at screening themselves, rather than asking the parents to do that from the information in the sign-up sheet.

Mention that a person who is a good match for role play is also a person who is willing to try something new or different, even if their first reaction is to say no. It's like at a restaurant and your mom or dad orders something strange. Will you try a bite? Just like this, in role play, you don't know if you like the role play (or the role) until you try it.

Finally, discuss "for the good of the group." Before this point was added, often there would be a group member who would not be willing to compromise or give up their (less than popular) idea for a role play. The point to make is that sometimes you have to give up your idea and go along with the group. Also mention that almost always such a person ends up enjoying the role play idea they thought they would hate.

Self-control

Self-control is the most important behavior for a role player to have. Respect is the most important attitude. Because the group is run by the kids, the group leader would prefer to not be the authority and use external discipline (of course not always possible). Understand that the development of self-control is a lifetime pursuit. One cannot expect children in this age range to possess consistent self-control. What is expected is a minimum of self-control *and* the demonstration of learning self-control by not repeating mistakes too often. A minimum of self-control means that, with a few reminders, a child shows progress toward not continuing to interrupt or distract the group or to draw attention to himself or herself and away from the group process. It also means the child can understand the importance of not being wild and is able to calm himself or herself if/when s/he becomes wild.

Earlier in the text, the term, "good match" for role play was used. As role play emphasizes the positive, saying that someone is bad for role play suggests something is wrong with the child. Rather, it takes a certain kind of child to flourish in the role play environment, so it is more of a good or bad match. A bad match for role play might mean a good match for the more organized groups of Scouts or a sport activity.

Length of Group

Usually, ninety minutes is a good length for an activity role play group. If this is an after-school activity group, consider some members may be dismissed a few minutes late. Also you may need to consider the time it takes to get to the role play room and to set up the room for role play. It is not uncommon to take fifteen minutes from room entry to finally getting a role play going, and early in the year, it is important to take extra time at the beginning to let the kids talk among themselves, that is, begin to bond.

It is best if the group runs for most of the school year, usually from mid- to late-September through most of May. While having two different groups where one would run from September until winter break and the other from January to May is possible, the leader would miss the enjoyment of experiencing and assisting the growth process over the whole school year.

Size of Group

Limit participants to eight children due to psychological considerations. The larger the group, the more difficult it is for the children to maintain self-control, to compromise to make choices, and the noise level is higher too.

Five members might be the ideal balance between a group that can bond and work effectively with each other and have enough members to do a variety of role plays. It is possible to hold individual sessions with as few as three participants (e.g., the flu might be making its rounds), making use of micro role plays.

Snack

The advantage of starting with a snack and talk period is to create group rapport and cohesion. On the other hand, some participants are excited to get on with the role play. Try to have the group make its own decision. Perhaps the members who bring snack must share a little with the other members, or ask them to eat snack while they wait for all members to arrive.

Animals

The issue is whether to allow kids to play animals within a role play. Allowing kids to play animals is not a good idea, particularly for the first half of the school year. With the goal of helping these kids grow psychologically, playing animals tends to do the opposite. Usually, it is a disguise for wanting to play younger children or those in need of being taken care of. While such a need is quite normal in this age range, doing it via animals tends to hurt the role play and the broader goals of the group, and it hides the real issue of not wanting to grow up. When this issue arises, call on their desire to be grown up by saying that playing animals is fine for first or second graders but not so much for you older kids. Then compromise by asking if perhaps that person would like to play a young child instead.

However, some groups can handle being animals, particularly after winter break. In such cases, require two things. First is that the animal can and does talk and walk on two legs. The second is that the child takes on the personality of the animal. For example, a cat would have extra desire to be clean, to like milk and moving objects and to be agile and coordinated.

Group Discussions

Children age eight and over can learn to carry on a group discussion (among eight kids) without raising of hands (most of the time). It takes some practice, and at first, it may appear to not be working, but the messages of maturity and cooperation this gives the kids are invaluable. The adult will most likely need to learn not to respond to raised hands. It is much easier to call on kids in the order you choose, but that message is that the teacher knows best. Since this role play group is the kids' group, leave it up to them who speaks when, and if a point you think is important is not expressed, then you are just another group member making a comment.

At first use, these conversations may be a little irregular; it's a new skill for this age, but they naturally want to learn it because it's more what older kids do. Be patient, and keep at it. Without punishment or consequence, remind the interrupter, and remind the rest of the group when someone is ignored (and discuss what the ignored person could have done to be recognized). After a few weeks, it will become the norm, and this skill could carry over into other settings, classroom and home. After three years of doing this, this writer still needs to slap his hand on occasion when he calls on a raised hand. The kids will learn to imitate this hand slap; just a quiet and light slap, more for the reminder than pain. For kids in this age range, they can understand the "automatic response" of hand raising to be almost involuntary, and slapping your own hand is a nonverbal way to acknowledge this. However, on occasion, you may need to get things moving (e.g., being near the end of group time), and kids seem to understand limited time as a good reason for being called on, while not expecting it in the future.

The Group Hug

Feelings can get hurt in role play, but with no insults or put downs allowed, the hurt is accidental. It could be physical, like when someone becomes overactive for a situation and knocks into another, but more likely it is psychological, an unintended hurt. When you see someone hurt and others are unaware of it, pause the group and point out someone is hurting, and ask the group to find out why, what happened. After talking it out, suggest a group hug, with the hurt person in the middle. You may find an initial hesitancy, especially among the boys, so the first time this happens, you may need to be more proactive (i.e., gently pushy) than usual to make it happen. This hesitancy is mostly related to (anticipated) feelings of embarrassment, but usually the kids *want* to do this. Usually, most of the same gender will gather around the hurt person (but you may have to encourage a straggler), in which case it is fine to have the other gender join in, making a circle, a second layer, of hugs. By the second or third time, all you may need to do is pause the group. They will figure out why and offer a group hug.

The only caution relates to the first and maybe second group meeting. You may need a little initial bonding for the kids to feel comfortable doing this. If it happens this early, you may just mention that you'll be teaching about the group hug next week, and that the person who was hurt is owed the first one.

Chapter 3

The First Group Meeting

The first meeting is unlike any other in that it is set out beforehand. By providing more structure, it is meant to relax the nervous child, to emphasize the need for organization (and not have a free-for-all), to provide the group leader with important information pertaining to tendencies of each child alone and in interaction with the group, and to give the group members an idea of what role play is all about and what is expected of them in terms of group behavior.

The first session sets the tone for the whole year. Some kids come quite nervous about what to expect. Begin by saying that this first group is different from what will happen next week, that today is mostly planned, but next week you will be making some choices about what role plays to do.

The first thing to do is to ask everyone to take a chair and to make a circle. Almost always the first circle is not clean. Some kids are a half chair out of the circle, and usually there are uneven gaps between chairs. This is the first example for them to use both self-control and to begin group bonding. Patiently ask them to make a good tight circle with everyone's knees almost touching (after group bonding, the knees begin to touch on their own) and with no one out of the group (or in the middle, as occasionally happens).

The sitting order in the circle of chairs is an important consideration. Often the members start off with the boys and girls sitting separately or with classrooms or friends clustered, but this does not encourage group bonding. Discuss whether clustering by gender is a good idea, but tell them that boy-girl sitting is required in role play in order to encourage group bonding. Suggest they see a role player rather than a girl or boy sitting on either side of them. The gender-split issue is normal in this age range, and you will be countering it whenever you can. If you see class clustering, bring that up for discussion. If you see two friends sitting or playing together often, mention to them that others may feel excluded from the pair.

Begin by asking who does not know the names of whom, and tell everyone to have a conversation to share and learn names, then ask if anyone wants to try and say everyone's name, which gives practice and can help capture a forgotten name.

Tell the kids that, at any time, they can choose to not participate and be an observer instead, but also ask them to try an unwanted role or undesirable role play before they say no. Any group member can choose to observe at any time. Vicarious learning, where an observer puts himself or herself into the role play via imagination, is a respected learning method. Some children may get more out of vicarious learning than actual participation. When necessary, teach them proper observing behavior; they are to sit to the side, usually against a wall and pay attention to the role play but not talk or interact in any way with the role players. Also, tell them they can participate at any time, but to come to the leader to help figure out the best way to (re-)incorporate them in the role play.

DISCIPLINE

Consistent with the philosophy of the group members controlling their own group, try to involve them in the discipline process. Preferably, there won't be serious problems because members already possess some degree of self-control. While patience is necessary in running any children's group, it is especially important here, because usually the administration of discipline results in loss of creativity which in itself is not a good outcome.

Many small not appropriate actions such as sitting on a table, talking out of turn, not keeping shoes tied, and running in the room are best handled with patient reminders. If these types of behaviors continue over several weeks, you could choose to use the "List of Mistakes." Simply, this is a tracking technique that does not involve punishment. On a piece of paper, write down the members' names in a column on the left, followed by column(s) for the target (mis)behavior(s). Each time a person does the behavior you are trying to stop, have that person take a pencil next to the paper and simply put a mark in the row of his or her name below the target behavior. When you describe this to the group members, emphasize this is only to track how many times each does that behavior, and there is no punishment. You can add that just keeping track of the number of times should reduce the target behavior. Research in psychology calls this monitoring of behavior, and it in itself can result in reductions or eliminations of the target behavior(s). You may find that some kids like to put check marks on the sheet, so emphasize it is a list of *mistakes*.

For all other misbehaviors, time out is quite effective. Being overactive or tending toward the hyper is the most common offense calling for a time out (or cool down time). Every week place an extra chair in the time out location, always against a wall and in view of a clock, but also in good view of the role play area because it's important the child on time out be able to follow the role play in order to rejoin the group. Describe to the kids that they are to ignore anyone on time out. Ask the child going on time out how long they think they need, and if it a reasonable amount, agree. Sometimes a child will suggest too much time. Ask that they time themselves and come to the group leader when the time is up so s/he can confirm their readiness and help them reintegrate into the group. On occasion simply tell the person to take as long as they need, and when they believe they are ready, to come to you. That is the best scenario. Rarely report time outs to the parent because it is best to work out problems directly with the child, which demonstrates respect.

However, if the problem is worse than that, or if it persists, then that person may not be a good match with role play, and at that point, the parent may need to be involved. Tell the child that you will be talking with his or her parent about this. Sometimes just the "threat" is enough to help the child to self-control. Ideally, it would be right after the group and where both parent and child can be present. Otherwise it may have to be a phone call.

SIX ACTIVITIES FOR THE FIRST ROLE PLAY GROUP

This preprogrammed first group is divided into six separate activities.

1. Rules and procedures. While these will vary according to your specific situation, discuss the importance of maintaining self-control, asking them for examples of self-control or the opposite. Mention that everyone loses some self-control every now and then, but maintaining self-control shows respect toward the other group members.

Require that every player has his or her shoes on and tied and has no laces on the floor. This is a safety precaution since group members do move around a lot. Go over off-limits areas such as the teacher's desk area.

Describe what their parents get, such as summary of what role play(s) and creative activities were used, but in general terms, with no names or identifying information. This parent memo is offered as a springboard for the parents to discuss the group with the child rather than asking for a full description of what happened.

2. Values. This is where you use appendices B and C, described with detail in the next section, Five Presentation Items. In this first group, you will use all of appendix B, but only some of the seven values in appendix C will be considered. Respect (appendix B) is the umbrella value under which all other values fall. There are three levels of respect: There is respect for the group itself and how it functions, respect for each group member, and, of course, self-respect. Discuss that respect means no put-downs or insults toward other members.

Continue by discussing that respect for the group means the group comes first. Discuss that you can't always get your way, that sometimes you just have to go along with the group, and that this involves compromise.

In this first group meeting, discuss patience (appendix C) because everyone, including yourself, will need it. Kids don't always stay focused on the role play (or the role), they will need patience with each other and themselves as they improve, and the leader will need the patience of an adult working with feelings in children. Just mention the other values and say you will discuss them next group. If they ask about I-CAG-WIW (I can't always get what I want), tell them.

3. Getting to know each other. Remind members that previously they did an activity to learn everyone's name. Make cross-classroom girl-boy pairs, maybe a threesome if there is an odd number of participants. If the group seems capable, just ask them to pair up, boy-girl, and not with someone from their own classroom. Start off with the brief creative activity of Mirroring, where, face to face, one moves slowly and the other follows, then they switch roles.

Then have a group discussion about what causes them to lose self-control, mentioning the positive flip side of what helps them maintain self-control.

4. Role play. This first role play, actually more of a scenario, has no assigned roles. Members play themselves so the leader can get an idea of natural tendencies such as who leads and who follows, who separates themselves from the group, who loses self-control, and the general interactive style of the members. Present them with this scenario: you go to bed at home, and you wake up on a sailboat in the middle of the ocean, with no adults, and there is a storm coming which you can see on the horizon. An advantage to using a sailboat is that members are restricted to a small area which encourages group interaction and even some conflict. Use chairs (facing out) to outline (i.e., limit) the boat dimensions, creating just enough space where members must make contact as they move about. Allow (don't suggest) the finding of land and getting there, and if it's going well, feel free to let it continue into survival skills and/or native contact. Stop it when it appears to not be adding anything new or you run out of time. As with most role plays, the resolution is less important than the process. Afterward, briefly discuss the role play, how it went and what they liked and didn't like about it.

5. Self-portrait (before and after). While self-portraits can tell a lot about a personality, without psychological training, they can simply be fun. Have the kids move two tables together (or enough desks for everyone, put together like one large table) and to bring their chairs over. While handing out pencils with erasers and a single letter size piece of blank white paper for each (tablets won't work for this exercise), ask them to write their name along the top edge (without specifying which edge is top), then ask them to draw a picture of themselves, not with a lot of detail, to take no more than five minutes, and that drawing skill is totally not important. While they are drawing, tell them that, near the end of the group in May, we will redo this self-portrait on the reverse side of the paper without looking at the one they did in September. Remind them that they will all be growing emotionally as they learn about themselves in role play (and outside of role play too), and that it will be interesting to compare the two pictures. Having them write their name is important. The first time with this game, more than one child did not recognize their self-portrait of eight months previous.

6. Circle story. As a closing game, the creative activity of circle story is fantastic. It can be very creative and funny, while at the same time requiring the kids to consider what the previous child said, add to it, and pass it on. You start the first one: I was exploring behind the school stage, and I found an elevator. I went in, pushed the only button, and it went down and down and down. When the door opened. . . . And that is where to pass it on to the next person who adds one or three sentences and passes it on, usually mid-sentence. This is a kind of structured creativity where members must work together to make a story which, however wild, makes some sort of insane sense. Several years ago, members created a chocolate tornado with Disney characters poking their heads out as they whirl around. Circle story is always popular and can be used as a closing game several times a year.

FIVE PRESENTATION ITEMS

Put these up on the wall rather than hand them out, and after presenting each the first time, put them up for a few weeks, and if necessary, as a reminder later in the year. Present them over a period of two to three weeks, usually in the following order.

First up is Respect (appendix B) which is used when discussing Values, the second activity in the previous section of Six Activities for the First Role Play Group. Respect can be seen as an umbrella value, covering all other values. Emphasize three aspects, and although all are important, they are somewhat ranked: Respect for the role play group, respect for each other, and respect for yourself. While many would see self-respect as the primary, over the years, and for this age range, this order of emphasis seems to work best. Respect for the role play group is the same as the respect required in the classroom environment, making the carry-over to the role play environment effective.

Respect is the first of seven values (appendix C), followed by patience, forgiveness, flexibility, understanding, communication, and I-CAG-WIW (I can't always get what I want, thank-you Rolling Stones). The following are notes related to each of the seven values. Usually present the first three in the first group, making reference to the other four, then discuss the latter five in your second group meeting.

Respect was discussed in appendix B. Patience is vital in many aspects. The group leader must be very patient while helping the children develop self-control and with many repeated reminders of common misbehaviors (feet off chairs, don't run inside, etc.), the children must be patient with each other as they develop a new role play idea, and they must be patient with themselves as they try to use self-control.

Forgiveness goes with making mistakes. Children need to forgive each other for intended (not allowed!) and unintended slights, and they need to learn to forgive themselves for being normal children who are being asked to learn some things many adults never master.

Flexibility usually draws a laugh with someone interpreting this physically. But, of course, this refers to emotional flexibility, to accept others with different personalities, to be willing to go along with a role play idea most others like but one may not, and the flexibility to try new things, to not say "no" before trying.

Understanding applies mostly to self-understanding, but also to understanding people different from themselves. They learn how to self-control, to work within a group that has a lot of emotion, and to begin to step out from themselves to understand there are other perspectives and opinions. Some role plays are geared just for this, for example, a role play about helping the homeless or where a child plays a parent of a difficult child.

Communication is, of course, vital to a successful group. This involves a child being able to explain a role play idea, being able to understand others' reactions to this idea, being able to say, with words, how one feels, and for other children to be able to understand said feelings.

While the Rolling Stones' song used the words, "you can't always get what you want," preferred here is the self-owning aspect of the "I" word. This is, of course, a valuable life lesson, and the kids enjoy saying I-CAG-WIW as well.

There is a presentation sheet for the three steps for role play (appendix D), usually reserved for the second session. These are, in order, choose the topic, identify needed roles, give/select roles to players. This is necessary because, almost always, as soon as an idea is identified, the kids start saying what roles they want, even before all roles are identified, sometimes before the idea is fully described. Emphasizing this procedural order helps in self-control, but mostly it teaches that there is a logical order to things, and it deemphasizes selfishness.

Also presented usually in the second session, there are two keys to role play (appendix E), keys that make role play work. First is to feel your character's feelings. Most likely, you will mention this frequently throughout the year. Second is to ask yourself, would my character say or do that? You may find that frequently you must remind the players to take the role play seriously (not necessarily for role plays that are primarily to "just have fun," as opposed to having a life lesson), and that "Silliness Destroys the Role Play." The latter seems to be most effective with the child who "goes for the laugh." Another part of learning delayed gratification is to not go for the joke at an inappropriate time.

A key phrase to mention is "for the good of the group" or "for the good of the role play." This applies to several aspects; going along with the group for an idea one or two members don't like (at first, but almost always they enjoy when they try), taking an unwanted role which is necessary for the role play to work, and for taking the appropriate role play seriously.

Creativity applies here as well. For example, if no one wants to play an adult in a role play needing adults, you could ask the group what changes can be made so no adults are needed.

Finally, recently added was another presentation item called Progress or Regress (appendix F), and this is used when the issue become relevant. *Pro*-gress is moving forward, and *Re*-gress is moving backward. Over the years, this leader has seen a subset of members who, every week, want to act younger than they are (and to take younger children roles). While they are most likely working out some personal issues, mostly they seem to stay stuck in that orientation. This also applies to the animals issue discussed in chapter 2. Establishing the value of progression helps the kids act a little older than they are, it helps with self-control, and in addition to the obvious life lesson, it seems to help the role play run better and longer.

Chapter 4

The Second and Third Sessions

Some groups come more ready for role play than others. Sometimes, with a little extra assistance, members can make up their first role play in the second group. Ideally, you will begin with members making up a role play, then you do one of yours (i.e., one from this book), have a group discussion, then if time, do a creative activity. You may or may not want to have a group discussion between the two role plays. As the group progresses from week to week, give them more and more control. While you should always come with ideas (enough to fill the entire time if necessary), it is better that new ideas come from the group members since it is their group.

Some groups may have a little difficulty getting going. Sometimes bonding (i.e., group discussion) takes over, leaving time only for a role play, or a member or two will have difficulty focusing (i.e., goofing off), or perhaps members don't yet grasp that the role play setup is just a beginning point and they have to find a way to continue the role play. Use your best judgment. Sometimes the extra bonding will pay off in coming weeks. You could discuss the need to focus, that it's not fair for the members ready to role play, and that self-control is necessary. If it continues, that means that member may not be a good match for role play. Mentioning this is usually enough to get any minimally capable role player to focus. See the subheading near the end of the next chapter called Regarding the Sharing of Fantasies for more information.

For the second and third meetings, you will want to have two primary role plays ready—a more organized one for a group with self-control problems and a looser or more flexible one for a group ready for it. You will also want to have a second role play, in case the group does not come up with one of their own. If you have a group with self-control problems, sometimes family scenarios can help.

For *family scenarios*, mention that we are going to do a few mini role plays where we have a mom and/or dad and one or two kids. Then ask the kids to make a semicircle of chairs (more practice in working together and the need for self-control to make a good semicircle) and to bring over two extra chairs which are placed facing each other in front of the semicircle. At this point in the group, it is best that the leader chooses who does which roles. While mentioning that a member can choose not to take any role they don't want to, remind them of the value of trying different kinds of roles. Choose a child and ask if they want the other member to be a mom or a dad. This is a good time to remind members that it is good when boys play girls and girls play boys. Then choose a mom or dad and describe the scenario. You want to get your parent to let you stay up later, to change your regular bedtime. After each time you do this with different players, label the strategy the child used (demanding, pleading, suggesting a compromise, etc.), then ask for volunteers to do it again. After two or three times, move on to the scenario of you want a raise in your allowance. Then add the twist of having both parents be present. Finally, perhaps add a fourth person for a sibling argument (e.g., who gets to play the video game or who gets the last cookie). Throughout, have the kids switch roles, sometimes between sentences, to give them a lively experience, to get them to take the other's perspective, and to begin teaching them role play techniques (e.g., switching roles). If the kids are enjoying this, have them make up some scenarios.

Chapter 5

The Role Plays

After these opening paragraphs, each of fifty role plays will be described, including the role play itself, necessary roles, variations, classroom variations, psychological implications, cautions, and notes about how it has worked in past groups. There is also a section for your notes as you use the role plays.

Role plays are listed from simple to complex. Early in the group process, favor the simple, and increase complexity as the group matures. If you are on a school year, the Christmas role play (You Are What You Get) can be considered the mid-point.

Implied is that simple role plays are better for the younger end of the age range while complex role plays will work better with kids older in the age range. But each role play can be adjusted toward the simple (e.g., eliminate a subgroup or simplify a theme) or the complex (e.g., add a subgroup or a theme).

SEVERAL CONSIDERATIONS

First, we will address several considerations when conducting role plays. These include use of electronics, four specific techniques, members' choice of role plays, choice of roles, during the role play, after the role play, an interesting philosophical summary of role play in terms of psychosocial considerations, and a discussion regarding the sharing of fantasies.

Use of Electronics

Over the past decade, the use of portable electronic devices (games, tablets, phones, etc.) has increased to the point where a new role play guideline is necessary. The use of any electronics, particularly cell, smart, and satellite phones, in any role play is not allowed, unless established beforehand. It is important that the role players solve problems themselves and not just call for help or an Amazon drone delivery. Role play is all about interacting with each other, not with electronic screens.

Four Techniques

There are four techniques which can be used very often. One is role *switching*, which is an excellent way to understand another's perspective and also teaches emotional (and logical) flexibility. When switching roles of players, ask that the last line be repeated by the person switching into that role. This helps to keep the emotional tone going.

Another technique is called *second voice*. This is where the leader might help a child express a feeling they are experiencing, but they are having difficulty expressing it, or it may be a way to guide the role play toward a psychological theme. To do second voice, stand directly behind and a little to the side of the role player and say a few words *in the role player's voice*. For example, a member playing a teenager is arguing with her mother about something, and the argument is not going anywhere. You might say, as a second voice, "let's ask dad what he thinks." This serves to progress the role play and to bring in more psychological opportunities for self-understanding, by adding another role to the mix. In this same scenario, if you thought there was still more to be gotten out of the mother-child interaction, you might second voice the teenager and say something about how frustrating it is talking to mom, or you might stand behind and next to the mother and say something about how hard it is to understand my child. Tell the group beforehand that when you use second voice, that person can either ignore you or take what you said and go with it.

Once this group leader let the group do second voice for each other, but he had to stop it because everyone wanted to try it. It was rather humorous watching second voicers being second voiced or to have multiple conflicting second voice suggestions being offered to one person.

Two other techniques are *freeze* and *pause* while a role play is in progress. Freezing means just that, literally freeze in place, but if someone is in an uncomfortable position, add "freeze, comfortably." Use freeze when you have something a little more serious to say to the whole group. It could be something as simple as the majority getting too active, or perhaps a player's feelings got hurt and s/he is crying, and you want to get the players to help that person.

Pause is a less intense stoppage. You might have a question for the group, like should we add a new character, or maybe someone wants to change roles and you want to get both the permission of the rest of the group and their understanding that a role has changed, or it could be something as simple as you asking if this role play is still working.

Members Choice of Role Play

While the leader should always come with a couple of role play ideas, it is good to let the group make up their own role plays, since it is their group. Making up a role play involves first being able to explain, with the right amount of detail (i.e., not too much) the role play idea, and second, it calls for a lot of compromise among group members. The kids learn the valuable lesson of needing to change their own idea so that a majority like it (or at least are willing to go along with the idea).

Sometimes a child might mention a movie or television show as a role play idea. This is not allowed because, one, possibly not all kids are familiar with the show and, two, it limits the creativity because some things, particularly the roles, are fixed. When this happens, suggest the child take the role play idea but throw away the show. So instead of using Princess Lea in Star Wars, the player might say a princess trying to do good things in an evil galactic empire. Yoda would become a generic wizard trying to help.

Depending on the group, at the beginning of the third to fifth meeting, you would simply ask, "what do you want to do today?" People begin suggesting role play ideas. While it does take some experience to have some understanding whether an idea might be workable, that is not always necessary. Part of role play is that it is okay to make mistakes. When a role play idea the group leader comes with does not work, s/he can admit to it being a bad idea, and we either change some elements in the role play to give it another chance or we start over with a new idea. It is helpful for the kids to find out a role play does not work and for them to explain why. Usually, role plays don't work as well when they get too wild or have insufficient focus, so let them experience that, then discuss what is needed in a role play to help with self-control. For example, with alien first contact, the emphasis is *peaceful* first contact, and that the goal is to understand each other. Before this element was added, the first contact would usually end up with one group chasing the other. They learn that anything that could result in a chase is not appropriate role play material.

Usually, there is more than one child with an idea. In this case, ask if there is a way to combine the ideas into one role play. Usually, there is, but if not, let the group decide which role play idea to use. Usually, they choose to use majority voting. But if there are about equal numbers for each role play, mention that almost half don't like the chosen idea and ask what can be changed to make it more appealing, or even go so far as to suggest they find a new idea that most people like.

When developing a role play, not too much should be set beforehand. Basically, you want a situation and some sort of peril or conflict. You are lost in a forest, and a storm is coming. A rock star is ready to perform but gets performance anxiety. An alien gets separated from his or her parents and ends up alone on earth. Setting up much more than this limits the creativity of where the role play can go. This flexibility allows the children to take the role play where their emotions need it to go.

After the first few weeks, the process settles down to making up a role play, followed by using one from this book, and concluding with a creative activity. But ask the group if they would prefer to make one up first or do one from the book first.

For this second role play of the day, you would reset your circle and discuss the role play, first identifying needed roles, then the members can choose their roles. Often the mood changes with the first role play, and it is possible members may want to choose a totally different role play to do second, so try not to set up two role plays at the beginning.

Flexibility is often called for; on any given day, you might have to give up or significantly change your idea based on the emotions the children bring. If you are not sure what changes to make, just ask the kids. After all, it's their group.

How the role plays listed in this book are presented is important. A good role play idea can be quickly rejected because it was not presented well. Once the kids have "no" in their minds, it's hard to get it out. Start off by naming the role play, followed by just one or two sentences of description. Be alert to, and try to incorporate, any suggested changes as long as the psychological meaning is retained. Letting the kids make some changes helps them own the role play, as they own the group.

Role play "fighting" is not allowed, partially because of the philosophy of the school where the group is conducted, but there is very little tolerance for this anyway. Thus, a role play idea such as knights defending a castle would need to be changed to something like the knights are invited to a Thanksgiving dinner and must suppress their "natural" urges. Emphasize the need for peaceful solutions and to use words instead of weapons.

The primary point of the children choosing their own role plays is that they must learn to work together and to consider the desires of all members in this process. They must be able to describe their ideas clearly. They must learn about compromise and the value of the good of the group, where someone might need to go along with an idea they don't like (which is also a good life lesson since most of the time the person ends up liking it).

With creativity, all the role plays can be adjusted for your group and its needs, both in terms of target age range (complexity) and content. The environment can be changed to best fit your needs on any given day (e.g., change the desert to the arctic circle if you are in a heat wave), roles can be changed due to interest (e.g., "we want to play teenagers today!") or what is needed (e.g., a less controlled group might call for changing parents into boarding school instructors and the home into said boarding school).

Choice of Roles

The next thing to do is to identify which roles are needed, and nearly 100 percent of the time you will have to remind the players that first we identify which roles are needed, then we decide who gets which role. The roles can be listed on paper, tablet, or white board in the room if necessary, but it also makes a good memory lesson to not write them down.

When more than one person wants a role, we have another learning experience. In this case, you might ask who would learn more from taking this role, or you might suggest that the person least like the role should get the part ("you're already a good leader; let someone else try being the king"). But in the end, it's up to the kids, and sometimes it comes down to something like rock-paper-scissors.

After the roles are chosen, it is important to set up the physical environment. The use of props is strongly discouraged in order to encourage the use of imagination. However, it is okay to use chairs as chairs or perhaps as barriers or walls. For example, two chairs side by side, with three chairs behind, makes a car. More chairs makes an SUV, van, or airplane. Three or four chairs forms a barrier between the girls and boys bedrooms.

Have the kids specify where are the key physical elements of the role play, for example, where is the trail, where is the village with the settlers or natives, where are the cooking and sleeping areas, so everyone can share a common fantasy.

You might find the need to add a role in the middle of the role play. For example, in a role play discussed later in this chapter, Adventures in Aftercare, an incident may call for a parent or perhaps the school principal or vice principal. You might have an idea who would benefit from this role and suggest who gets it, or you might leave it up to the group to decide.

During the Role Play

Finally, ask exactly when does the role play start, for example, before or after the storm which destroys the settlers' supplies. Then simply say, "Lets do it!"

During the role play, the leader is actively walking about, trying to keep track of everything, which is not always possible, in which case you can simply ask, what is happening? Try not to meddle too much, but be ready with suggestions to make the role play move ahead, to try to bring subgroups together, and to encourage any psychological themes to support self-understanding and personal growth.

Finally, about five minutes before it is time to end the role play (either it's the end of the time together or you think an ending creative activity might be a good idea), tell them they have five minutes so they have an idea of when they will need to leave their fantasy, and also to give them time if they want to end the role play with a conclusion.

Be sure to emphasize the process of the role play over its resolution. Usually, role plays don't actually end, and the kids usually don't mind that at all. Sometimes it is as simple as saying, "oh, here's a way out of the trap."

After the Role Play

It is a good idea to have at least a short group time at the end. If there were psychological themes, or if a child had some strong emotions, this is the time to discuss how the role play applies to real life. For example, after a role play about being lost at the mall, you might ask if any of the players had ever been lost from his or her parents and how it felt. Or you might mention where a role play went bad and what they did to fix it.

Often you can end the group with a creative activity, some short and some a little longer. The choice depends on a combination of how much time remains and what you think the group needs in terms of their emotional tone and self-control (e.g., something calm for an overactive group). Usually, they enjoyed the circle story from the first session, so circle story is a popular choice. Chapter 7 describes twenty-seven creative activities which have been popular over the years.

Finally, depending on your environment, you may get a chance to meet some or all of the parents when they pick up their kids. You may not meet the parents of kids who are going to aftercare, but some parents will be waiting for their kid. Meeting a parent can be educational, to see how the child relates with the parent and siblings, and it is also fun to talk about role play with the parents. But remember confidentiality; talk in general terms, and if you want to share something specific with a parent, try to ask for the child's permission first.

On occasion you might feel the need to share something specific with the parent, usually due to the child having some sort of recurring problem in role play. In this case, try to talk with the child first, saying that you think it is important that it be discussed with the parent, then try to have the child there during the discussion with the parent.

Philosophical Summary of Role Play in Terms of Psychosocial Considerations

There is a subset of psychosocial factors in common with almost all the role plays. First, the players gain experience in working with others (communicating, compromising, mediating, sacrificing for the good of the group, etc.) in a flexible (i.e., give and take) and fast changing environment of their own making, with as little as possible adult control. This leads to self-understanding and also interactive social understanding, although it is often difficult to separate the two. Second, flexibility of imagination is also in common for almost all the role plays; things can change very fast so that one needs to be ready to give up one fantasy for another. There are no or few actual props to limit imagination. Third, the desire to be independent and the desire to be protected and cared for are both very common psychological themes in this age range. The uncomfortable feelings related to learning independence can enhance the desire to be protected; at this age, children can bounce back and forth as they strive for mastery. Many role plays target these twin needs. Fourth, the concept of leader-follower is pervasive. Even if not required by the role play, often someone takes the leader role. Providing feedback in real time is particularly valuable here, mostly in terms of the frustration of players not following the leader and of the leader being less than effective (e.g., the level of assertiveness, or too pushy/not forceful enough). Encourage the kids who don't want to lead to go ahead and try leading.

Regarding the Sharing of Fantasies

Sometimes in a new group, even after all the explanations and considerations of what role play is all about, one or more members just don't "get it," or more accurately, choose not to respect "it," that is, the philosophy and basic procedures of role play. Often it is someone who just wants to play and not be bothered with the structure or limits inherent in a shared fantasy, or perhaps someone who does not understand that it takes some focused effort in order to have fun in role play. Sometimes a child might be impatient with other kids who have some difficulty learning to do this. Usually, this becomes evident after a couple of role plays go for a few minutes then fail because no one knows what others are doing. The members start off at the same place, but then the fantasy diverges into whatever each child or small subgroup of children desire.

In appendix B, we established that Respect for Group is most important (followed by respect for each other, then respect for self), and appendix E focused on two ways to make role play work; feel your characters feelings, and especially, would your character say or do that?

One of the most valuable lessons learned in role play is how to be creative within the limits established in the role play. If you have a role play set in the past, a helicopter cannot swoop in to save the day, because it just does not fit within the role play boundaries. As does snow or McDonalds on a deserted desert planet. Or suddenly becoming a Ninja during a restaurant scene. This illustrates one of the primary differences from free-time fantasy play where just about anything can happen if desired.

   The key here is that role play is a *shared* fantasy, and in order to share a fantasy, there must be boundaries and limits as well as the sharing of information. And since it is their group, primarily it is up to the members to correct each other in terms of the boundaries or limits and in the sharing of information. Of course, the group leader might want to get this process going with some feedback, but primarily it is up to the group to stay within the bounds of the shared fantasy. Labeling this process as "focusing" on the role play can help in this age range.

   During a role play, members should feel comfortable suggesting to someone that what they are doing or saying does not fit in the role play. It's better for this to come out immediately from a peer when an off-topic action is about to occur, rather than having to back up and redo something that could otherwise have made the role play lose focus and direction. When someone wants to do something new, it is vital that s/he ask all others in their subgroup, so people know what is going on. If the role play has two subgroups (e.g., humans and aliens), then sharing information is vital within your subgroup, but some information may be valuable to share with everyone. This sharing of information helps with some kids who withdraw from the action because they lose track of what others are doing.

A Note for the Listing of Role Plays and Creative Activities

The role plays described in this chapter, as well as the creative activities in chapter 7, are listed, with overlap, from simple to complex. Simple role plays are better early in the group process, and the more complex role plays are better done later in the group process, after the group has developed its own personality and means of working together. If you follow the school year, the Christmas role play (You Are What You Get) can be considered the break point of winter vacation.

   There is some arbitrariness in the order of the listings. Some role plays and creative activities have similar complexity levels, and some variations in preference and ability can be expected in terms of the makeup of the role play group.

   Every role play can be adjusted toward the simple or complex to fit your needs. The typical way to simplify a role play is to eliminate one of the subgroups or to simplify or eliminate an element. Complexity can be provided with an additional subgroup or by adding a new aspect or theme. When making adjustments for your needs, only the underlying theme, as described under the "psychology" subheading, should be maintained.

Candy Store

Description: One person is the owner of a candy store. The players enter the store and line up at a table which is the serving counter, with the candy behind the counter (so children have to ask rather than taking themselves). Each player puts on a personality and can choose an age when asking for candy. The store owner also chooses a personality. Switch roles frequently so all who want to be the store owner can do so.

Roles: Store owner, children of various ages.

Variations: Maybe think old-fashioned store with ladder behind serving counter and candy all up the wall in giant glass containers. Suggest the owner make a big deal about getting the candy.

Classroom Variations: Use as is, since it teaches appropriate school behaviors. For older children, replace the candy store with another type of store (clothing, video), but ask them to choose the type of store.

Psychology: This role play begins to teach the importance of "putting on" personalities, and it reinforces waiting patiently for your turn and respecting others by being quiet while in line so they can hear the interactions of other customers.

Cautions: Emphasize being consistent with your personality because usually the kids don't. Keeping them in line also helps keep the activity level manageable, but that might come as a suggestion (via second voice) from the store owner ("I can't serve you unless you are quiet and in line.") or another customer.

Notes: Usually have this role play early in the school year because it helps the kids learn about putting on personalities and because it does not require a great deal of group cohesion. It is an easy and fun role play suitable for your first group.

Your notes:

Wake Up in Campground with Adults Gone

Description: The players are themselves at their current ages. They went to bed in their tents with everything fine, but they wake up in the morning and the adults and car are gone. You can choose whether or not the food is also gone.

Roles: All players play themselves. Adults are needed only if the players create them, such as a camp ranger.

Variations: None; there is specific psychological content in the design of this role play.

Classroom Variations: The teacher disappears, all the doors and windows are locked, and the phone does not work, so the class is on its own. What do they do? You may have to restart this scenario if the class goes for uncontrolled and wild behavior, perhaps asking how the quieter students felt and why the wild students ignored them.

Psychology: Practicing independence is the primary theme, but with more emphasis because there are no adults, at least at the beginning. Also taught is planning before acting and to do this planning in a group. It is often illustrative to see who (if anyone) steps forth to be a leader.

Cautions: So far, kids always see this as a challenge, but if a child becomes frightened, maybe ask if someone wants to be an older sibling, or suggest the frightened child play a teenager. Sometimes kids want to focus on finding out why the adults are gone. This should be redirected to what the kids need to do now (find food and shelter if the kids find those gone, or find a way home).

Notes: This role play focuses on the desire to be independent among children of this age range and to solve problems without the help of adults. The challenges of being independent are important to this age range, and this can be discussed after the role play. Always mention that adults would not do this for real (but the kids know this already).

Your notes:

Campout Disasters

Description: While on a campout, Things Happen, such as floods, earthquakes, and the food disappears (also see Wake Up in Campground with Adults Gone).

Roles: Depending on player preference, the roles will vary. Usually, the kids play themselves, but any needed role can be added in process, such as parent, camp ranger, police, rescue squad, and the like.

Classroom Variations: Combine a role play with your disaster drills, focusing on what would happen if the drill was real.

Psychology: Learning to cope with problems, often without adult help, gives the kids a chance to feel self-confidence in the face of threats.

Cautions: Don't allow roles that can result in chases, such as large animal attacks, or in interpersonal violence, such as a Bad Person.

Notes: The school where this author conducted his role plays has a strong environmental emphasis. They go out twice a year on multi-night learning experiences to gain firsthand knowledge about nature, biology, history, geology, and the like. It is possible that in schools without this emphasis that this role play might hold less interest.

Your notes:

Submarine

Description: Be it kids on a field trip or scientists exploring the ocean, submarine role plays usually are popular. What happens depends on which focus the kids want and the roles they choose. The key element is that the players start off in a confined space. Use chairs facing outward to outline the boundaries of the submarine. Make it just large enough so that people can pass, but with touching.

Roles: Often, it is school kids on a field trip, but it could be a family, a group of scientists, or even treasure hunters.

Variations: You can vary by the types of roles which were just described.

Classroom Variations: Not possible in all classrooms, but suggest you are going to hold the next lesson on a submarine. Move the desks as close together as possible (so they can't get in or out), and continue with a class lesson. After a while, have them move back and discuss how the new layout affected feelings and behavior.

Psychology: The narrow confines of a submarine force the kids to interact more with each other, and with the leader's emphasis, the threat level can be heightened, for example, by limited air.

Cautions: Try to keep the kids on the actual sub for as much time as they can handle. They may want to go outside, so make a big deal about getting ready to do that, checking each other's gear.

Notes: When they go outside, have them use the buddy system in order to increase interactions.

Your notes:

Ages

Description: Role Players lay on the floor, separated so that no one can reach another. Start off by saying, you're in your mommy's tummy and about to be born, then right away, say you are now being born. Every little while, shout out a new age, each age older than the last. Give them time between each age, depending on what you see them do. Start the aging process by saying, you are two months old, then go quickly through infancy; six months, one year old, two years, three years, then five years old. Let them stay at five for a minute, then in about two year increments, get to their own ages, then start asking them to be one, two, and then three years older, then go to adolescents, spending some time at thirteen, fifteen, and then eighteen. Mention they are young adults now. You may pause and ask what they are doing in their lives, then start increasing by about five years until thirty-five or forty, then ask them what they are doing for a living. Don't worry about their occupations making sense. Then go up in ten year increments. Keep going until anyone who is going to die does so. There are sometimes some who refuse to die. Finally, have some fun jumping back and forth between widely differing ages, such as eighty, five, forty-five, nine, and so forth, until they appear to have had enough.

Roles: The kids play themselves.

Variations: With older kids, possibly do it twice; once saying your family is poor and homeless, then again saying your family is wealthy, then discuss differences.

Classroom Variations: On a day when the class learns about careers, have children start as in twelfth grade and continue into adulthood, while asking career type questions.

Psychology: Children enjoy the moments when they have permission to be younger again, and they enjoy the idea of being older and having a sense of mastery. They also love jumping back and forth between widely differing ages, and this gives them experience in being versatile. One can make the case that effective people can be different ages depending on what is called for, so it can be considered a life skill.

Cautions: Don't take much stock in what they say they are doing for their jobs as adults. Anyone younger than high school rarely has that clear of a vision of themselves into the future.

Notes: This is a relatively short role play and can be used as a creative activity instead. No one has yet asked about how a baby comes out of mommy.

Some kids already know the facts, and others appear to not understand yet, but don't dwell on it unless someone brings it up. In discussion, you could ask them what their favorite ages were and why and discuss any trends or interesting things you observed.

Your Notes:

Halloween: Haunted House

Description: On the group meeting before Halloween, read this to the players in a deep formal voice:

I am House. I have been here since before the American Revolution. Many families have come and gone from Me. I grew upset because people kept on leaving, so one day long ago, I captured two children to stay with me, forever. I like children, so I made it so they would not grow up, never getting older. But now they say they want friends.

Then tell the role players they are going house to house on Halloween and come to a long and dark driveway. They feel driven to walk up to the house and ring the doorbell. Also tell the two players chosen to be the captured children that they want to go out and experience the world. Remind the other players that the two captured children have been alone in the house for over 200 years, and ask them where they think the kids might like to go.

Roles: Two play the captured children in the house, and the rest play themselves.

Variations: After the "trick or treating" kids show the captured kids around, if there is still interest, have the captured kids show the other kids around the spirit world. Ask them what regular kids would want to see in the spirit world.

Psychology: This role play has the same aspects of The Lost Children role play. Being lost in time allows for the mastery of blending into today's world.

Cautions: Beware to stop any chases. Emphasize the desire to know each other over scaring each other.

Notes: You may want to give some suggestions about where to take the two kids, places like they have never seen before such as an ice-cream store, fast-food restaurant, or an amusement park.

Your notes:

Halloween: Lost in Cemetery

Description: Kids get lost in a cemetery at Halloween night. When they read a tombstone, that person rises up out of the grave. They then talk with them, take them around to see what they want to see, then convince them to return to their grave.

Roles: Kids and the people who rise up out of the grave.

Variations: When the person rises up out of the grave, the player becomes that person. All the players' ghosts go out to see what changes have happened in the world. Maybe individual players could have a conversation with the kid who caused him or her to rise up, where the player takes both roles.

Psychology: Playing a dead person seeing a newer more modern world addresses feeling out of place. Observing yourself is a new skill for these children.

Cautions: Remind players of the seriousness of this if they start to get silly. Talk with a player if s/he rises up someone they actually knew who died.

Notes: The players' choice of grave risers tend to fall into two categories, historical figures and imaginary figures, even combinations of imaginary figures (e.g., a combination of Barney and Barbie).

Your notes:

Halloween: Next Year!

Description: Ghosts, goblins, and similar characters chosen by players meet to discuss how to frighten the kids next year. They test out their ideas (a role play within a role play).

Roles: Ghosts, goblins, and the like as chosen by players, little kids.

Classroom Variations: For older kids, say they provided a Halloween haunted experience that ended up being too scary for little kids. Have them plan for next year, to make the scare level just right.

Psychology: Discussing how to frighten little kids is like discussing how to frighten yourself, and both doing it and having it done to you helps children deal with fear.

Cautions: If there does not appear to be enough action, emphasize the part where they test out ideas.

Notes: None.

Your notes:

Aliens, First Contact!

Description: A group of aliens have landed in a deep forest on Earth. The humans are a first contact team sent to investigate and make first contact. The role play begins at the human camp site near the alien camp. The group as a whole (all role players) silently approaches the alien camp, hiding together in one group behind trees to observe the aliens. The group converses in whispers and discusses what members see, until they create a common image of the scene, both the setting and what the aliens look like. The group then quietly withdraws back to its camp to briefly discuss and plan for first contact. After planning, the group chooses some to play the aliens. The rest of the players return and make first contact.

Roles: Alien contact team and aliens. In the contact team, younger kids can choose to play adults or children, while older kids can create specialties such as scientist and linguist.

Variations: The primary variation is in how many play aliens in the contact part. There should be at least two people in either group. This mostly depends on how many members want to be the aliens.

Classroom Variations: Instead of humans and aliens, use new and established students. Due to class size, the two groups should be split beforehand, rather than everyone participating in the observation part. Plus, all dialogs should be spoken loud enough for everyone to hear. The established students group together in a corner while watching and commenting upon the new students in their new habitat (i.e., working and talking). Remind them they must be respectful. When the established students withdraw to plan first contact, the new students should be able to listen in on the plans, but making no comments. Any class split could work. If the class is having gender-based issues, the split could be males and females. Perhaps tie this in with a lesson by having the students split into the subgroups of your lesson. But always, the goal is *peaceful* first contact.

Psychology: The observation part teaches how to create a common fantasy that is internally consistent, and it also teaches how to keep your voice down while passing on complex information. In the contact part, members learn to communicate nonverbally while challenging their preconceptions. What could a hand shake or a smile mean to an alien?

Cautions: It is common for the first contact to turn into a chase. If you see this happen, first emphasize it's *peaceful* first contact, then ask the group running away what the other group did to make them want to run, then ask the other group what they were actually trying to do.

Notes: Usually the contact part is redone in different ways, particularly if the chase develops. If you switch roles to start over, usually it is best to skip the observation part and begin at first contact.

Your notes:

Adults Forget How to Take Care of Themselves

Description: You wake up as children in the morning, and all seems too quiet. You go to breakfast and find no one in the kitchen. You go to your parents' bedroom to find your mom still sleeping, but when you wake her up, she knows who you are but not that she should make breakfast, or even how to make breakfast. You have to teach her how to do everything, like how to make breakfast, drive you to school, and when to pick you up.

If the role play goes well, suggest other things like, it's a weekend instead and it's time to choose a family activity. If dad gets added, he has the same problem as mom. Ask role players for other situations.

Roles: Mom, maybe dad, and children.

Variations: You play the parent. In this variation, you can add logic to the mix, for example, the kids teach you how to drive but don't tell you where to put the key, or you can enhance some life lessons by, for example, asking "why go to all the trouble of making breakfast when I can just give you this candy and cake?" The problem might be that you have six or eight kids trying to teach you stuff, in which case you might have one of the kids play your spouse (gender of kid is irrelevant because kids understand the concept of having two moms or dads) and ask some of the kids to teach him or her.

Classroom Variations: The teacher forgets how to teach, so that the students must teach him or her and perhaps do some teaching as well.

Psychology: Taking care of parents is self-empowering, like switching roles, so that the child is the parent, particularly when the kids teach something they learned how to do recently like simple kitchen tasks. Children can learn, and reinforce what they have already learned, by teaching others.

Cautions: If the kids play the adults who forget, don't get bogged down in doing things the "right" way. Instead, accept the illogic of kids, and go onto the next task.

Notes: If the kids enjoy this role play, perhaps suggest the variation of the teacher forgetting as a separate role play for a future week.

Your notes:

Wig and Brush

Description: Imagine a huge statue of a person, tall enough to almost fill the length of the room if it were laid on its back. While pretending that the statue is standing up and surrounded by scaffolding, the players actually crawl along the floor to climb the scaffolding. Like "day for night" in the movies, the pretend here is "horizontal for vertical."

The town people have decided the statue head is ugly and needs to be helped with a giant wig. Divide the group into two subgroups, and simultaneously have one group gather hair and make the wig, while the other group makes two giant brushes to use on the wig. Although you ask who wants to be in which group, in reality, the boys will most likely choose to make the brushes, while the girls choose to make the wig. Although cringing at the inherent gender bias, this is as intended, since it is mostly a gender lesson.

After each group makes their parts, then everyone together places the wig on the statue head and combs it out. Getting this massive object from the ground to the head takes teamwork, then some people will need to hold onto the wig while others are combing. There could be a discussion before-hand about how to style the hair.

Roles: Girls and boys.

Variations: It could be any activity that naturally divides by gender and con-cludes with everyone needing to work together. Require people to work in pairs for additional teamwork practice.

Classroom Variations: Use as is, but probably make the role play shorter and the discussion longer.

Psychology: While focusing on gender issues, also pertinent is working as a team while maintaining the "horizontal for vertical" fantasy.

Cautions: Kids will forget about gravity and the scaffolding and may need to be reminded. Maybe have everyone wear an imaginary rope. If disorga-nized, ask them to choose a leader.

Notes: Continue to mention the massiveness of everything; humongous head, whopping wig, bulky brushes.

Your notes:

Wake Up in Another Environment

Description: This role play can be similar to the role play used in the first group session (wake up in a sail boat with a storm coming). The players choose the environments. While possibilities are endless, some of the more interesting environments suggested have included wake up: in a dumpster, during pioneer or dinosaur times, when earth began ("like when there was no ground or anything!"), in the middle of a big city, on the moon, or in a classroom with a lesson in progress. This is a convenient way to make up a role play when "starting from scratch" did not work.

Roles: Usually have them choose a common narrow age range, for example, their own ages or a couple of years older, so as to encourage interactions, but sometimes the roles are suggested by the environment (e.g., wake up on the moon suggests astronauts).

Variations: Split the group into two, and have half each wake up in different but nearby environments, with the stipulation that the groups combine resources.

Psychology: Learning independence is primary, exemplified by having to cope with a strange and unanticipated environment, usually with no adults to help. Also, practical skills can be learned when you must take care of yourself.

Cautions: It can get wild, so watch out for the usual traps of chases.

Notes: You can suggest environments too.

Your notes:

Pyramid: Get Trapped and Explore

Description: Explorers decide how to get into the pyramid (secret or open entrance), do so, then get trapped where many strange things can happen. Usually, the players come up with the perils. More than once the kids came up with narrow passages with trap doors, a king or some treasure in the middle, hidden rooms, and an ancient caretaker or Cleopatra (or her ghost).

Roles: Explorers and anyone they discover inside. The kids can decide if they are students or adults.

Variations: Players can be people who were placed in the pyramid when created, and they must find a way out, maybe even meeting explorers trying to get in.

Classroom Variations: See the Under the School role play.

Psychology: The key considerations are mastery in dealing with this situation and creativity to make the journey interesting and difficult.

Cautions: Leave it up to the players to come up with what happens inside, unless they are low on creativity that day.

Notes: It seems that almost every year someone suggests a pyramid role play, so this is listed by popular demand. But then, almost anything can be found in a pyramid (even a "mummy of my mommy"), leaving the adult a lot of leeway in creating psychological or fantastical material.

Your notes:

Stranded on an Island

Description: Be it tropical, desert, arctic, or wherever, the players get to
    the island via some calamity (e.g., shipwreck, plane crash) which is also
    enacted. The goal is to get the kids to focus on survival, that is, coopera-
    tion, gathering food, making shelter, and finding a way home. The addition
    of a native tribe is common, at which time some players switch roles to be
    the natives.

Roles: The captain/pilot (and possibly cocaptain/copilot) of the vessel that got
    them there, and a group of other people (e.g., a family, kids on a field trip,
    and even scientist/explorers).

Variations: Add the element of someone shipwrecked years ago.

Classroom Variations: See the Quest role play, the main focus being on bond-
    ing, planning, and working together.

Psychology: Enacting the crash or ship sinking serves the subconscious pur-
    pose of working on how to respond to real past or just imagined memories.
    Focusing on group survival involves group planning and working together.
    Also there is a strong theme of learning independence.

Cautions: Limit the amount of time they spend on getting to the island, that is,
    preparing the boat or plane and the crash itself, because otherwise they will
    likely spend more time on this than working together to survive.

Notes: Clearly establish where the shore line is. Often players use all the
    open space for the crash, so the space may need to be repurposed. To
    make the role play run more smoothly, describe the two (crash and island)
    environments before the role play starts. If natives were added, specify
    their village.

Your notes:

Rag Doll/Teddy Bear

Description: Divide the group in half. Half go to the toy store to buy rag dolls or teddy bears (each player chooses which), and the other half are the rag dolls and teddy bears. They take them home. The dolls/bears have minds of their own, but they can only move and talk when the humans are not around. Their goal is to go out and see the world. They try to manipulate the kids into doing this.

Roles: Half are children, and half are rag dolls and teddy bears.

Variations: Alternately, the dolls/bears want to go out on their own without the children. Maybe have the dolls and bears, with the humans, visit the rag doll and teddy bear factory.

Psychology: The independence theme is multifaceted in this role play. The dolls and bears are trying to become independent, the human kids are serving as adults to the bears and dolls, and then they can work together to explore the outside world. Also, the dolls/bears, by doing things behind the kids backs is like the children doing things behind their parents' backs, and the players get pleasure in doing so.

Cautions: It is usually best that the kids bring their dolls/bears to their bed-room, so when they leave the room, the dolls/bears can move about, talk, and make plans in private.

Notes: The dolls and bears have a lot of fun freezing when the children return to the room. Tell the players that, after a while, the dolls/bears make some mistakes so the humans figure out they have minds of their own (e.g., the humans come back to the bedroom to find the dolls/bears have moved ever so slightly), or else the role play will not move ahead. You don't need to suggest how the secret is discovered; they will come up with that themselves.

Your notes:

Space Station

Description: Players are scientists in today's space station. They can reenact the launch and boarding the station. Emergencies always happen. Decide beforehand some activities and what can go wrong. Space walks are always dangerous, so require the use of the buddy system.

Roles: Scientists.

Variations: Maybe add a rich tourist or some other unlikely role.

Classroom Variations: 1. Transform this into a scientist in the space station answering questions from your class. The scientist needs to be one of your more imaginative students, and the answers don't have to be realistic at all, as long as they make sense to the class asking the questions. 2. This one, more like a creative activity, might be fun for some classrooms. Divide the class into groups of three to five students. Ask them to imagine how gravity helps when you poop. Remind them this game needs to be done respectfully. Ask each group to design a zero-gravity toilet, then have them present their ideas. End with a description of the actual toilet used on the space station.

Psychology: Mastery and leadership are themes. If a leader does not naturally step forward, wait a few minutes and ask the group how it is going without a leader.

Cautions: In order to focus the role play, come up with some background peril, such as oxygen is leaving the earth, so the space station scientists need to find ways to help the people of earth cope. Also, if there is a tourist, s/he needs to be taught how to do things such as move around and eat.

Notes: Add roles as needed, such as people on the ground. Have some players play two roles. Emphasize moving around with no gravity.

Your notes:

Wrong Way Restaurant

Description: A family goes out to a family restaurant where things go wrong. After seating the party, the waiter takes orders back to the chef where s/he misinterprets anything possible, while meeting the letter of the order. The waiter returns to serve the food. Examples of misinterpretation include hamburger (a slice of ham between buns), milkshake (bring a glass of milk then shake it in front of the customer, of course, spilling it all over), spaghetti (one strand), meat loaf (a cow just laying around). Ask for a soda and get a soft drink (liquid in a pillow). Ice cream Sundays may only be available one day a week (and may be noisy because of the I scream!).

Roles: Waiter, chef, customers. Optionally, someone may want to play the cashier, but suggest this is a small role at the end so they also need another role.

Variations: In theory, it could be any type of business; however, food lends itself nicely to these misinterpretations.

Classroom Variations: Two students are directing a class play. Have them spend about five minutes alone creating the theme of the play and the setting of one scene. They are to direct four other students, and these students try to take literally what the director says but they get it wrong. This is a kind of language game where the director must learn to be specific (e.g., "stand over there and act sad," and the player goes way off stage, behind some object and starts crying loudly and dramatically). The players get to be creative while still doing what the director says. See also Rulers and Servants which uses the same language loophole idea.

Psychology: A common fear among children of this age range is making mistakes, particularly as they are just testing independence behaviors. It is self-empowering to have the adults making the mistakes instead and fun to be allowed to make such mistakes.

Cautions: The customers may tend to leave their seats. While that is okay, try to keep them in their seats at the appropriate times, such as when ordering and eating.

Notes: Using a restaurant also encourages dramatic interactions among customers and exchanges between restaurant staff. Redo the role play, reassigning roles, if there is interest. Enjoy the food combinations they come up with, such as pasta that talks back (thus, someone gets an additional role of playing the pasta).

Your notes:

Skyscraper

Description: A skyscraper is being built and is almost finished, so there are
walls and floors, but not much else. Players must start at the top and work
their way down to the bottom. Each floor holds a different problem or challenge, made up by the players. The person who created the floor environment leads the challenge for that floor. If the player does not want to lead,
ask that they make their floor passage brief, as little as two minutes, while
some floors may have more elaborate issues. Usually, each player leads his
or her group across the floor to the opposite side or corner.

Roles: They play themselves, except for roles called for by the challenges.

Variations: Let the players decide how finished the building is; just stairs or
elevator, finish floors or open gaps, external walls or not.

Psychology: This role play incorporates some elements of the Fear of Heights
role play, but mostly it calls for members to cooperate in planning and
implementing ways to get through the challenge. If a member comes up
with a unique fear, ask if that relates to a real experience they had.

Cautions: None.

Notes: Examples of challenges include floors of jungle, fractured fairy-tale
characters, pitch black with large hole in middle, broken staircase, tropical storm, wind, lawyers (it was funny, really), and floor of fast changing
emotions.

Your notes:

What Am I Feeling?

Description: Split into two groups. Give a different emotion to each group, and give them time to make up skits which portray each emotion. Then each group takes a turn displaying their emotion while the other group tries to guess what the emotion is. After the first few, have the groups choose the emotions themselves. Usually, create a semicircle of chairs for the audience. Discuss other ways you could have portrayed that emotion.

It is also possible to give the same emotion to both subgroups and focus on the differences in presentation.

Roles: As needed by the skits.

Classroom Variations: Use as is, but limit the groups to four or five students so everyone can have input.

Psychology: Illustrating emotions is a way to better understand them and to own them.

Cautions: Some groups may not want to do fear and related emotions. Remind them of the values of approaching the uncomfortable and of self-understanding.

Notes: Examples include anxiety or tension or nervous, feeling left out, confusion, annoyance, feeling over- and underwhelmed, as well as the staples of happy, sad, joyful, depressed, and lonely. This same process of "each group does a skit on the same thing, then compares," is used in The Same Message role play.

Your notes:

Family with Spoiled Children

Description: Two parents take their kids out for dinner, followed by a trip to the toy store. Start the role play outside the restaurant (i.e., skip the trip).

Roles: Two members play parents. Two of the kids get to be spoiled, while the rest are "normal." More than two spoiled kids gets too wild and impossible for two adults to handle.

Psychology: Playing the spoiled child gives the player an odd sense of mastery, since they tend to exaggerate the spoiled aspect beyond what they would ever do themselves. It sets up a cognitive dissonance between the fun and guilt of misbehaving. Those playing parents learn some of the frustration when dealing with a child acting spoiled.

Cautions: You may need to give permission to act spoiled; it's surprising how often the child self-limits in this role because s/he knows it's wrong in real life. Then again, you may need to tone down the portrait of spoiled to something somewhat reasonable.

Notes: Of course, discuss being spoiled and how it is selfish, perhaps mentioning to not try this at home.

Special Note: For groups with older kids, after the end of this role play, there is a good opportunity to teach a little psychology, specifically the concepts of id, ego, and superego, if you feel comfortable doing so. The spoiled child brings out the id ("I want this NOW!"), while the parent represents the superego ("No, you have enough toys already.").

Have two kids stand side by side and play the id and superego roles. Suggest the topic of candy because it's a great example. Ask the id and superego to discuss whether to eat candy now, then ask how do we choose? Then ask for a volunteer and place that person in between the id and superego, calling it the ego or negotiator. Ask, what could you say to get both sides to be okay with the final decision? Your goal is to bring out something like this: Id: "I want candy now!" Superego: "No. You'll spoil your appetite for dinner." Ego: "Maybe have one piece now and save the rest for after dinner." Finally, mention that all three parts are inside all of us, that we have this discussion inside but are not always aware of it, and that it applies to a lot of things, not just candy. If you remember in the following week or two, if examples come up during role play, reinforce the learning by reminding them.

Your notes:

Fear of Heights

Description: Players awake on the top of a skyscraper being built. It is just girders and a few boards to walk around. Walls, floors, and ceilings have not yet been put in. Together as one group, they must get down to the ground.

Roles: Members play themselves, unless one, for example, wants to play a construction worker there to help (but let that suggestion come from the group).

Classroom Variations: This could be a good group bonding experience early in the year.

Psychology: Confronting fear when with peers is a special situation, especially if acted out with real emotions.

Cautions: Let anyone who wants to watch instead to do so, but be ready to integrate them back into the role play if it appears they are ready.

Notes: Keep emphasizing, if necessary, that they are on top of a "naked" building, maybe add wind if they don't have enough fear. Emphasize the need to work together, to not leave someone behind, and if they don't on their own, ask if they should elect a leader.

Your notes:

Magic TV

Description: You change the channel of your living room television, then you climb into the TV to experience it, then exit the same way. Repeat, usually for each child to choose a channel. Only nonviolent situations are allowed. In each channel room, roles can be repurposed so some play the role of the show's characters while others are the visitors.

Roles: The kids usually play themselves and characters in the TV.

Classroom Variations: Call it magic door. Create a door through which one can enter another classroom at another school (or grade level). Have them focus on different types of schools (private-strict, private-relaxed, boarding, religious, Montessori, etc.), and have them reflect on the differences and what they like and dislike about each. If possible, use a member who has actually attended one of the types of schools in order to help with realism. End with a discussion about different methods and environments in which to teach.

Psychology: This role play has limited psychological implications, but it can be a lot of fun. There is the usual give and take when choosing a channel and roles, particularly unwanted roles (see the Notes section of this role play). This role play does call for a higher degree of working together, and you can limit the space of the "stage" inside the TV to encourage this.

Cautions: Remind the kids about the rule of not using extant shows, movies, or characters but instead allow them to use those environments but with different characters. Players can play themselves in the environment. But if everyone knows the TV show, then it might be okay to use it that way.

Keep aware of time and interest level. You will probably need to say something like, "in three minutes we need to exit the TV for the next person" to keep things moving.

Notes: This is a good role play to emphasize taking a role the player does not like, because it's only for a few minutes and not for the entire role play. If the child ends up liking the role, be sure to point that out to the entire group, so you can remind them if needed in the future.

Your notes:

Cultures

Description: Two very different groups from very different places meet over dinner to share their cultures and perhaps discuss and work through a disagreement. Usually, divide the group in half, and each group spends ten to fifteen minutes planning their culture by setting up one or two behaviors, traditions, and two foods. Each group prepares a meal for the other. If the group wants, beforehand set up an area of disagreement to discuss and resolve after dinner. Add entertainment from each culture if desired.

The cultures could be extant on earth, or could be not human and come from an alien planet, or perhaps one of each.

Roles: As chosen by participants, but no little kids.

Classroom Variations: This can be used as is. However, if you have a bicultural class, perhaps have representatives from each meet and discuss something like choosing a theme for a party or prom. See if anyone wants to play a member of the other group. The culture split could be done by gender, perhaps stipulating the school is moving to unisex bathrooms and how would they design them and make rules for use.

Psychology: Creating an internally consistent set of behaviors, traditions, and foods helps foster intercultural sensitivity and appreciation of others. Being asked to present one's culture, and having a culture presented to them, provides a good contrast and suggests understanding differences as a way toward self-understanding.

Cautions: Make sure each group's set of behaviors and traditions are internally consistent. While the two groups are creating, ask each group separately to describe to you briefly what they plan, and make comments as necessary.

Notes: Allow more creation time if they are into it. The cultures can be made up.

Your notes:

The Lost Voice

Description: In the middle of a class presentation at school, the child loses his or her voice.

In addition to the school setting, maybe include trips to the doctor, hospital for operations, recovery at home, visits from friends, or as chosen by participants.

Roles: The voiceless child, older and younger sibling, parent(s), doctor(s), hospital staff. Extras play peers, first in classroom, then friends visiting.

Variations: When the child comes home, his or her sister or brother also loses their voice.

Classroom Variations: Instead of trips to the doctor and such, keep the role play in the room and have them deal with it. Maybe do it near the time you are preparing for a drama presentation. Students would need to use alternate means of communication to continue the play or skit.

Psychology: At this age, there is some fear about suddenly loosing something like one's voice. The role play is about fear and coping with fear, particularly in relation with others.

Cautions: Be sure to discuss fear at the end of the group, how it happens, how people cope.

Notes: None.

Your notes:

The Lost Children

Description: Two children are lost, and the rest of the players form a group to help find the lost children. Usually, leave it up to the group as to whether they help the lost children get back home or instead learn to adjust to their new environment. Some groups will want to enact the getting lost part, and that is fine. While this is usually set in a forest, in the city would be an interesting choice.

Roles: Two lost children, the rest play themselves and other roles called for as the role play advances.

Variations: A variation is to have all players except two being lost. Another variation, more of an enhancement, would be, of the two lost children, one could be meek while the other could be strong. Among the rescue party, there could be two assertive people who both want to lead.

Classroom Variations: Instead of a lost child, you have a new student who must learn to feel comfortable in the new environment. This would be more of a discussion than a role play.

Psychology: Being lost, or feeling lost, is a common fear among children just starting to want independence. This role play allows for the lost children to either be cared for or even for the lost children to decide to go off alone after being un-lost by the other members. The meek and strong personalities and the two assertive leaders bring in the issue of assertiveness. Combined discussion of assertiveness and feeling lost can be valuable. The variation where all but two children are lost allows for a feeling of mastery by the two children who feel the responsibility of taking care of several other children.

Cautions: Try to help the lost children actually feel lost, or else it becomes more of a game with less psychological meaning. Maybe talk a minute with the lost children to find a time in the recent past where they felt lost.

Notes: It is important to have a discussion after this role play, because it can bring up some painful memories. Share something from your past if you can, and help the group members share their experiences of feeling lost and of the outcome, that is, how they were found.

Your notes:

Under the School

Description: There is something special hidden under the school, something the teachers and principal had built, and they use it in secret when the students are gone. Let's find a way in, go, and explore it, and maybe we will find an adventure or two down there as well. Under the school where this role play was developed, there exists a bowling alley, and amusement park, and a jail for naughty kids. Create things down there that relate to your school and its staff.

Roles: Members play themselves, possibly with personalities.

Classroom Variations: Design an educational theme amusement park, using colored markers and poster-sized paper. Divide the class into groups and have them first specify the educational theme, then brainstorm ideas, and then create fun rides and interactive displays to teach the theme.

Psychology: What is under the school may be a representation of one's subconscious. If you evoke basic emotions such as fear (e.g., from a roller-coaster), being lost or being hungry, deeper emotional themes may manifest.

Cautions: Try to keep the kids in one group or two subgroups that combine and split as you progress (e.g., "What is that in the shadow? You three go check that out, then report back").

Notes: What is under the school, and how you get there, depends on your environment. Getting there is some of the fun and is dependent on what can be found in your role play room. This leader's role play room has an electrical outlet in the floor, and the security cover has a small raised circle on it. They were told they must "spaghettify" themselves (a term coined by Stephen Hawking of what happens to humans as they begin to enter a black hole) to fit through that little hole (which just happens to be the diameter of a piece of spaghetti). You may need to be creative in finding the way in, including asking the kids to find it. The back of a closet is always an option. Also, while setting up some things you might find under the school, leave room for the kids to make up their own things where adventures can ensue.

Your notes:

You Are What You Get (Christmas)

Description: Usually set as a Christmas role play, it can be any holiday where presents are given, even one made up, such as Present Day. The kids open their presents, then they become their presents. No violence-oriented toys such as guns or swords are allowed. They must deal with situations created by the players. Thus, when all presents are open, you pause the role play to review who is what and to create scenarios appropriate to this mix of "present" characters.

Roles: Kids play themselves when opening the presents, but, of course, then they take the role of whatever their present is. If the present is an animal or a stuffed animal, the player is required to play that role on two feet and using words, while taking on the personality of the animal.

Variations: Yours to discover.

Psychology: While there is little native psychological content in this role play, some presents and combination of presents may suggest something.

Cautions: Political correctness, or even just respect for group members, may suggest using a non-Christmas theme.

Notes: Try to add psychological content to the "present" role. For example, if one person got a toy dinosaur, you might ask if it is a veggie-thaurus or a meat eater, and you might suggest the dinosaur is conflicted because it is a meat eater that does not believe in eating meat. It might be up to you to create opportunities of psychological meaning, but the kids may get the idea and come up with some of their own.

Your notes:

Adventures in Aftercare

Description: While two kids play adult day care workers and step out of the room, participants make up various day care scenarios which must be dealt with when reentering the room. Redo so all have a chance at playing adults. The two players wait in the hall and must deal with whatever is presented when they reenter the room.

Roles: One supervisor, one assistant, and the rest are kids, usually age eight to ten, but occasionally as young as preschool. Possibly a parent might be needed.

Variations: The kids love it when you take a turn in the hall and they must set up a situation for you. Do not fear if you don't handle it well, but feel comfortable in admitting it. You should take your turn after all the kids have played adults, and emphasize the situation needs to be realistic, since you won't be there to help develop the scenario.

Classroom Variations: See the role play Deal with It!

Psychology: The kids reinforce their past learning by making up situations for the "adults" to deal with, and the "adults" enjoy the challenge of not knowing what to expect and of solving a problem like an adult. Mediation is the learned skill when the adult must deal with the needs of multiple children, as is understanding how difficult it can be for an adult.

Cautions: Sometimes the person playing the supervisor does not lead, and you may have to describe that the supervisor can tell the assistant what to do. Do not call it day care, because the kids may interpret that just for little kids. More so than other role plays, it is important to keep the scenarios realistic, and this should be emphasized as you help the kids develop scenarios.

Notes: This role play is a favorite and is well liked by participants. You set up the first scenario. Perhaps give two things to deal with at once, so you might set up an argument at one table ("Jane is taking all the red markers and won't share!"), and when the adult(s) come over to deal with that, another child comes up and keeps trying to get the attention of the adult talking with the arguing kids ("help me tie my shoe! Now!"). Other popular scenarios include the kids are playing first graders waiting in line to go outside and one child is not able to get his shoes tied, a child is too loud, a new child is shy and does not know what to do, a child or two children don't admit to leaving out a game, someone cuts his or her finger, and a child is hiding in the closet and does not want to come out. After the first few situations, the kids make up the scenarios.

Your notes:

Rulers and Servants

Description: One or two players are rulers, and the rest are servants. The rulers give commands, and the servants follow the *letter* of the command but get things wrong when possible. The servants try to find the loopholes in the rulers' commands so they can get them wrong without "meaning" to.

Roles: Rulers, servants. Usually the two rulers are of different genders so as to include everyone, and that encourages more gender interactions.

Variations: For older ages, require that two rulers agree on any command and for servants to decide on a common response or set of responses.

Classroom Variations: Rather than conduct a full role play, tell the class that you will be listening closely to what they say, and you may misunderstand if what they say is not clear. This can teach how to be specific in speaking and can be a fun challenge for you as well.

Psychology: Some of the pleasure kids get out of being a servant is they get to better the adults. Some of the challenge of playing a ruler is to be precise in using verbal commands. This is a particularly good role play for the child who does not want to lead to get experience being the boss and to discuss this concept in general.

Cautions: Following this role play would be a good opportunity to discuss the concept of equality and respect for a person, regardless of job or position in life.

Notes: Switch roles so all who want to can be rulers. Usually, the players need a little direction at first. As an example, a good command to use is "make me a pizza." This can be correctly (mis)interpreted as turning the ruler into a pizza, making a pizza the size of a penny, or putting absurd things on the pizza such as a toaster ("you've heard of toaster pizza?"). If a child does not want a turn at playing a ruler, suggest s/he does it with another person, so that any command must first be decided between the two or that s/he be ruler just for three minutes.

Your notes:

Principal's Office

Description: One, two, or (occasionally) three children get in trouble in the classroom and are sent to the principal's office.

The role play starts in the classroom with someone playing the teacher. The kids usually decide on the behavior that gets them sent to the office, and that is acted out. Use simple low-violence things like pulling of hair, a poke in the back, or making a mark on someone's work. There is a witness. The teacher escorts the kids and witness to the office (a nonextant assistant stays in the classroom) where the core of the role play occurs. After a talk, the principal calls the parents in for a discussion with their kids present.

The witness is a wild card and should be a level-headed player. Tell the witness s/he is to make up what was seen, but that your choice should not be biased in favor of either kid who got into trouble. The witness is a new role in this old role play, so use it as you think best, or not at all. Everyone else will have to quickly adjust themselves to this witness' information, which is good practice for life.

Roles: Principal, parents, witness, classmates, teacher. Most players have multiple roles; first as classmates, then as principal or parent. Some usually just watch and learn vicariously.

Variations: If the person in the role of principal has difficulty with the role, you can suggest that a vice-principal be created to help the principal.

Classroom Variations: Use as is.

Psychology: Acting out "wrong" behaviors, then being held accountable for them, is something children this age gain a lot from, sometimes at an subconscious level. They enjoy being empowered to play adults dealing with their child's misbehavior. And they may have to flip their thinking based on what the witness says.

Cautions: The person playing the principal should be one of your better role players. It is a key role that can make or break the role play.

Notes: None.

Your notes:

Tiny Troubleshooters

Description: When a big person can't do the job, call on the tiny people. This idea came from Fantastic Voyage, where people and their ship are miniaturized and injected into the blood stream of regular (big) people.

Roles: Roles depend on what the job is.

Variations: Yours to discover.

Psychology: The concept of a tiny person fixing something that a big person can't fix addresses the common independence theme in this age range.

Cautions: There has been mixed results with this role play idea. Some of the problem may lie in imagining the big people in the role play.

Notes: Make the big people roles both very clear and more appealing, or else no one will want to play them. However, it is easy to adjust the role play so that no big person roles are needed. Some job ideas include a surgeon needs help in fixing something inside a big person, a plumber can't find the leak or the item dropped down the drain, the black hole is so small that only tiny people can go through, and building a circuit board to help with their own memory or other ability.

Your notes:

Deal with It!

Description: One member steps out of the room. The rest then choose a scenario which the member must deal with. Scenarios can be wide ranging, and can be both short and long. Complexity of scenarios can vary by age and ability. Here are some examples.

- You are on a crashing plane, or there is a tornado or earthquake in progress.
- Someone says: The school called me to say you had a problem today?
- You are here to be interviewed for the position of child (youth) president of America, and we are the interview committee.
- Everyone stands up and is really glad to see you. They ask, where have you been the past three years?
- You are a seventh grader who has been asked to join a teachers' meeting to discuss reducing the amount of recess time during lunch.
- You are a visiting teacher to teach us Introduction to Spell Casting.
- You are here to ask us to give money to your cause. What is your cause, and why should we give money to it?
- Everyone bows his or her heads and asks, "Master, what is today's lesson?"

Roles: The persons stepping out of the room plays themselves, and the rest play roles appropriate to the scenario.

Variations: Possibly two players step out of the room.

Classroom Variations: Two students step out of the room, and the class sets up a situation that involves misbehavior or something going wrong appropriate to the classroom.

Psychology: The concept of not knowing what you might be confronted with at any moment is not seen as threatening by the role players, but rather they enjoy the feeling of mastery in dealing with the unknown. The creativity in developing scenarios under time pressure is a good learning experience for life situations.

Cautions: Be quick in choosing scenarios so the person in the hall does not get impatient. This also teaches how to be creative while under time pressure.

Notes: This role play is similar to the role play Adventures in Aftercare, but with different types of scenarios.

Your notes:

Space Camp

Description: Modeled after NASA space camp for kids, the players are aboard a mock space shuttle, but the shuttle actually launches by mistake. The kids usually want to start the action as they climb into the space vehicle.

Roles: Commander, copilot, navigator, scientists, and possibly ground control.

Variations: Possibly loose communication with the ground so the players must solve this without adult assistance.

Psychology: The mastery of taking care of yourself while in a scary environment is key here, as is being a leader or a follower.

Cautions: Label the tasks each role must do and specify scientist disciplines because the kids won't have a good idea. Keep them on task, that is, getting back to earth. Usually, they will want to explore, so keep this part as real as possible.

Notes: This has been done with and without ground control, and preferred is without ground control so the kids must solve the problem without adults. Also, if they want ground control, maybe the role play leader could take this role, because kids don't have a realistic understanding, and you playing it will keep the kids on task. Unlike many role plays, this one actually has an end. Maybe you could also play the ground commander who gives medals out to these amazing kids.

Your notes:

Imaginary Friend

Description: The role play starts while in your discussion circle. Ask members to move their chairs outward a couple of feet so "someone" has room to stand next to them between the chairs. Ask each child to choose or create an imaginary friend, either his or her actual imaginary friend if s/he has one, or someone who they admire (real or imaginary, dead or alive), standing next to them. The only limit is that his or her imaginary friend will need to be able to talk. Everyone introduces his or her friend to the group, describing them however each wants, but each must include some words about his or her imaginary friend's personality and how s/he is feeling right now. Then everyone becomes (switch roles with) his or her imaginary friend.

The first task is to pull in the chairs as they usually are for group discussion. Tell the players they just had a conversation with each other about their imaginary friends. Now that you *are* your imaginary friend, have a conversation with each other about your "real" friends. Do what you can to keep the conversation focused on feelings and not silly topics. Interesting topics may include: What do you think of your "real" friend? How does your real friend treat you? What would you like to do that your real friend does not want to do? Do you like what your real friend chooses to wear to school or what they choose to eat?

Then move to action. Form the chairs into a semicircle and give each, one by one, a topic with which they can have a disagreement conversation with their imaginary friend. A good one is, do we do the chore or do we go out and play instead? For each member's turn, have them jump back and forth between his or her imaginary friend and themselves and actually carry on a conversation until resolved. Make sure each actually turns around, back and forth, while conversing, and for those with the ability, encourage use of different voices and personalities. Each member can do the same disagreement or make small changes such as what chore, which makes for better comparisons between coping methods.

Roles: The child and the imaginary friend.

Variations: The primary variation is how much conversation and how much action. Some groups may prefer one over the other, so after a while of conversation, ask if they want to move to something more active or to make up more conversation topics.

Psychology: The imaginary friend is considered a projection of some aspect(s) of one's inner self or subconscious personality. Interacting with your imaginary friend is another way to have a conversation about your-self, with your self.

Cautions: Keep focus on feelings, and avoid silly as much as possible. Look-ing into one's subconscious can be uncomfortable, so humor is important.

Notes: In this age range, many kids will not be able to separate the personali-ties of their selves from their imaginary friend. During the conversations and action, note when kids actually show the different real and imaginary personalities.

Your notes:

The Same Message

Description: Divide the group in half. Choose one message, with some psychological content if possible. Each group has about five minutes to create a skit to act out the message. After both groups perform their skits, everyone discusses how and why each message was different. After a while, have the players make up messages.

Roles: Dependent on how each message is presented.

Variations: After dividing the group in half, give each subgroup a different message, then see if the audience group can say what is the message. Note this substantially changes part of the psychology behind this role play, although comparisons can be made between how each group portrays similar messages, or one group may do the other group's message later on in the role play.

Classroom Variations: The variation would be only in the messages you provide, and they can be related to what is currently being learned (equal gender rights might suggest a message of "men and women are equal"), or to classroom issues ("reading helps your future").

Psychology: Participants learn creativity and cooperation by working on how to present the message, but primarily they learn that things can be different but still be equal.

Cautions: None.

Notes: Message examples include eat right, eat wrong, it's easy to hurt a feeling, peace is better than war, help the homeless, become a cheerleader, become a robot, and it's okay to make a mistake. This same process of "each group does a skit on the same thing, then compares" is used in the role play What Am I Feeling?

Your notes:

Special Powers R Us

Description: Each child has a special power but also a related weakness. As a group, they use their powers to help those in need. Have the kids make up their own scenarios, but ideas include a child is afraid to come out of a cave, people are trapped in a submarine, something happens on the space station, a volcano is erupting, someone lost his or her job and his or her family is homeless, and fires in skyscrapers or homes. Emphasize working together to solve the problem, especially if a combination of skills would be helpful.

Roles: You will need to spend time developing each player's power and related weakness. Although it is best if the kids make these up, some examples to draw upon include power over another's thoughts and/or feelings (maybe the weakness is that you have to take their thoughts and feelings so that, the more you use it, the more confused and emotional you become), power to move inorganic objects (while it becomes more difficult to move yourself with each use), power to shrink things (but you can't return them to full size, and you get smaller with each use), power over the weather (but maybe the wind increases with each use), and power over time, making it run either fast or slow (but with each use you become a little more lost in time, exemplified by you slowly fading away). You don't want to use your power too much because it drains your energy.

Variations: Maybe split the group into two, and say they have to share power between groups to make anything work. You can have identical powers and weaknesses between the subgroups or complimentary but related powers, such as one can make time run faster, but their counterpart in the other group makes time run slower.

Psychology: First there is the empowering aspect of having powers. Second, there is the concept that everything comes at a price. Third, it is also empowering to help others. Fourth, players must work together (either in one group or two subgroups) to solve problems.

Cautions: The kids may want to over-use their powers, making it more of a contest of who can out power whom, so keep the focus on helping those in need.

Notes: If two players want the same power, and you are using one group, require them to both agree before using their power.

Your notes:

Strict Boarding School

Description: Players go to a strict boarding school, with separate bedrooms for those players choosing to play boys and girls (establish one bedroom for each gender). They begin by moving in (setting up their bedrooms), then go to dinner, followed by evening activities (or free time if your group has sufficient self-control), breakfast, and then perhaps the classroom.

Roles: Players play themselves mostly. This is one role play where you will want to take the role of house mother or father, and possibly instructor, in order to make it more realistic and to keep them on target.

Variations: Instead of a classroom setting, use gym or art class, which a student can lead realistically.

Classroom Variations: Perhaps create a "detention school" and have the kids set up the rules and what is taught and how it is taught. This would be more a talking than acting exercise.

Psychology: This is more a "feel good" role play where the kids can express independence. Try to bring up for discussion how it might feel to be sent away from home, the good and the bad, since that is an underlying theme as well.

Cautions: This may not be a familiar environment. At the beginning, you may need to talk a little about what a boarding school is (like summer camp but at school). Make it clear that it is not military school because some players will see that as an excuse for using violence.

Notes: In order for the kids to take this role play seriously, it is important that you play an adult for some of it at least. As house mother or father, the kids need to interact with you at various times. Every time this role play has been done, the players would want to sneak out after bedtime. You might let them (by falling asleep in your chair) but catch them coming back. Having you as an adult will be necessary for the meal time scenes to work. The activity level of your role should reflect the needs of the group; if they are less self-controlled, you will be more strict and more interactive. Don't hesitate to switch roles if someone wants to try leading.

Your notes:

Summer Science Experiment

Description: One player's parent said the group could use their garage work-shop on a summer day to make something. The kids first decide what to build, then they build it, but then, of course, things go wrong. Encourage the kids to discuss what can go wrong ahead of time. If desired, regroup, discuss, improve their designs, then rerun the experiment.

Roles: Everyone plays themselves but are encouraged to put on personalities.

Variations: Divide the group in half and each creates something different, but in the same workshop so they must communicate. Maybe suggest the two creations must be things that will then interact. A variation for older kids would be the role play Human Robot.

Classroom Variations: Tie this in with another lesson. With the class, choose a science experiment that creates something related to a current lesson. Divide the class into groups of five to eight kids and have each subgroup create their experiment, then recreate it in front of the other groups. Clearly, their descriptions will be of key importance. You can assess how well they understand the lesson behind the experiment by how they use the knowledge in creating/describing the result.

Psychology: Cooperation in creating a common fantasy is important, as is consequences when the experiment has problems.

Cautions: This role play has a tendency to become overactive, so be ready to make some on-the-fly adjustments.

Notes: It is key to have input in what is created. It should be something that can go wrong, such as a weather experiment that goes out of control and creates a hurricane or shoes that walk on their own.

Your notes:

Tree House

Description: Your parents said that you need to learn how to live by your-selves. They gave you lumber and building tools and one day of food. The players build the house, move in, buy food, and maybe get jobs. Add perils such as a wind storm, or a lost child shows up. If (some of) the players do get jobs, try to make that an issue in the day-to-day life.

Roles: Players play themselves but add personalities if they like. You might ask if they think having a leader is a good idea, if no one steps up to that role. The lost child is always a good addition that (as described in The Lost Children role play) provides much psychological focus, both in terms of being lost and in helping the lost child.

Variations: There are many possibilities such as an older sibling who makes fun of the tree house or who wants to join the fun, grandpa or grandma wants to have a look inside, and what food to eat.

Classroom Variations: School House—all schools are closing, but you still need to learn in order to pass the state achievement test, and parents are not allowed to do the teaching. Have one or more subgroups of students design their own school, focusing on what is taught and how it is taught.

Psychology: The feeling of mastery comes from solving your own problems and living without adult help. Working together is a strong element, and if the group decides to have a leader, there is psychology there.

Cautions: None.

Notes: Expect the players to splinter into one, two and maybe three person sub-groups, and when they do, that is a good time to bring up whether to have a leader. Each subgroup can be given different tasks. This role play naturally segues from the building and getting jobs to living in that environment.

Your notes:

The Queen (King) Is Senile

Description: The queen or king is senile. She has two children (prince and/or princess), each of whom has a personal servant. Other roles as needed; guards, cook, performers. The focus of the role play is for the children to compete to get on the best side of the queen/king, in order to become queen or king. Each child, with his or her servants, tries to find out what the king/queen wants then try to create and/or give it, all in the hope of being chosen as the next leader.

Roles: Queen, king, two children, two personal servants, other roles as needed (guard, cook, performer).

Variations: Genders can be totally mixed; two kings or queens and two children of the same gender. If you have a player who likes to play a child between five and seven years old, make that person the much younger child of the queen and king. This added dimension could prove very useful if the prince or princess decides to use the younger child.

Psychology: Learning good and bad ways to present yourself and seeing some of the consequences is a direct life experience. Getting on the good side of the queen or king is like doing the same with parents and teachers. Playing a failing leader is like playing the parent while getting things wrong, something few children fail to enjoy.

Cautions: Probably you will need to describe what senile is.

Notes: Discuss the methods used to get on the good side of the leader, which worked better, and which did not. Ask if the methods used are like what the members use with their parents and teachers.

Your notes:

Farm Animals

Description: Farm animals from a mean farmer who treated them badly are taken in by a new farmer who is kind. The role play usually starts with one scene of meanness before moving to the new farm. The "mean" behavior should be simple and not too bad, like being too strict or not caring about the animals' needs.

Roles: Farmer and farm animals.

Variations: The kind farmer could have a child who maybe is not mean but is disrespectful.

Psychology: The underlying message pertains to the range of simply not getting your way to mild child psychological mistreatment. Experiencing both the mean and kind increases the contrast between the two, thus enhancing the child's understanding. Playing the mean farmer has strong psychological implications, and it should be discussed at the end of the role play. Talk about how it felt to be the mean farmer, how it felt to be the kind one, and of course how the farm animals felt under both owners.

Cautions: When playing animals in role play, as usual, require the animals to walk on two feet, to talk human, and to take on the personality of the chosen animal. While it is possible that a member may talk in baby talk, this should be discouraged because it hurts the role play.

Notes: None.

Your notes:

Kid TV

Description: Kids create a television show for kids. Modeled after the local TV news, the anchor presents each segment. Segments are decided by participants, usually including in-the-field reporters, a weather segment, a sports report, celebrity news, and how-to and call-in segments. The latter can be very interactive.

Roles: Anchor, field reporter, the person about whom the field reporter is reporting, meteorologist, sports reporter, in-studio reporter, and other roles depending on what segments are desired. Possibly a camera person is used, but that is a nontalking role. Players usually experience different roles as the news progresses.

Classroom Variations: The TV show is school based, and reporters report on school activities, perhaps adding rumors (but be sure they use fictitious names), how to study, how to pretend to be paying attention to the teacher, and so forth.

Psychology: This role play has less of a psychological emphasis, unless a segment calls for it, for example, a field interview of a hero child in the hospital who pulled a child out of a wrecked car before it exploded. However, there is an underlying message, that kids can do adult things just fine.

Cautions: If someone wants to be the camera person, ask them if they want a backup role if one becomes available, in case they grow bored with it.

Notes: In-the-field reporter options can vary widely, from reporting about a pig farmer with new methods to make the pigs happy (you could also interview a pig) to interviewing the creator of a new roller coaster about how that ride is different from others. How-to segments have included how to bake a cake, wash your pet, and turn your stuffed animal or action figure into a robot. The sports reporter could create a new sport to report on. Phone-in questions could be limited to asking about the how-to segment just completed or it could be anything like "how do I get my dog to eat my homework."

There has been a Kid TV segment on more than one show over the years on PBS and Nickelodeon.

Your notes:

Quest

Description: Designed for both the younger and older ends of the target age
range, members must pass through natural obstacles to reach their goal.
When presenting this idea to the kids, read appendix G out loud with them.
Each child is strongly encouraged to take his or her turn as leader for one
of the obstacles. If you have less than eight participants, have the group
decide which obstacle(s) to skip. Then have them choose who will lead for
which obstacle, then do it.

Roles: Kids play themselves but can choose personalities to put on.

Variations: Described in appendix G are versions for the younger and the
older ages.

Classroom Variations: This could be done in the classroom as a bonding
exercise and also a way to teach brainstorming and planning before action.

Psychology: This role play calls for working together in one group with no subgroups. This is an excellent opportunity for personality traits to be revealed
in behavior, so if you feel comfortable giving feedback to individuals, be
ready ("how come you didn't say anything when the group was making
plans?" or "did you notice when you were leading the group that you ignored
Billy?"). Although the goal of the quest should have meaning, even if it's
rescuing your kidnapped parents, usually the players get involved in the
quest itself, with the goal having little effect on their feelings or actions.

Cautions: This role play requires a higher level of self-control than most others. Save it for a day when your group is ready for it. Sometimes it helps
to mention the week before that next week you will be bringing a role play
that requires more self-control, so be ready for it, then remind each player
when you first see them on the target role play day.

Notes: Your challenge is to offer the right amount of help to kids making
their plan.

Your notes:

Role Play: Create Characters Then Scenario

Description: Usually, when creating a role play, members create the scenario first, then identify the characters needed in that scenario. In this role play, begin by asking the players what roles they want to play. Ask them to be careful because they won't be able to change their choice after the role play starts. As with all role plays, don't allow violence-prone characters. Write down the roles on a white board, tablet, or on a piece of paper. Then, along with the group, create a scenario that can incorporate all the characters. You may find as this process advances, some members may want to change characters, and that is okay as long as it's not too disruptive in terms of what you have decided so far.

Roles: As decided by players.

Variations: You could take a few minutes to come up with a scenario to present and adjust per their feedback.

Psychology: This depends totally on the created roles and scenario. Not knowing ahead of time, your goal could be to provide feedback so the roles and scenario have psychological meaning. You could state that the scenario you all come up with should have some psychological meaning.

Cautions: Someone may want to change his or her role late in the process. While this can be disruptive, try to limit the change so as not to need a change in the scenario as well.

Notes: This role play gives the trained a way to flex their psychological skills, while the less trained can just have a lot of fun creating the roles and scenario.

Your notes:

How to be a Dummy (and Ventriloquist)

Description: Form into pairs and have each pair decide who will first be the dummy. Give someone two dummies if you have an odd number of players. The ventriloquist stands just behind and slightly to the side of the dummy and places his or her hand on the dummy's back or shoulder. It is important to physically touch your dummy because it increases the sense of the dummy having no will. This is how conversations are carried out:

1. The ventriloquist asks the dummy a question or makes a comment which invites a response.
2. The ventriloquist whispers the dummy's response into the dummy's ear.
3. The dummy must say exactly what the ventriloquist said, and with the same emotion.

When describing this role play, it might be a good idea to mention that, on television or the stage, usually ventriloquist acts are comedies, but in role play, it should be more like a normal conversation with feelings.

You can talk with your dummy about anything within the guidelines of appropriateness. Avoid being silly. Commands should be practical and doable. For example, telling your dummy to perform a back flip is not practical, but checking the knee reflex might be. Discussions should be real and somewhat personal, as though you are talking with a real, feeling person. Maybe you and your dummy can talk (respectfully) about someone else like a teacher, mom, dad, sibling, or friend.

Then switch roles and do it again.

It is vital that the conversation remain respectful, polite, and positive, with no plans of violence or making fun of or hurting anyone.

After a while, try two or three pairs of dummy and ventriloquist. Have the dummies talk to each other, or other between-pair combinations. Maybe the child plays his or her mom, dad, or teacher and talks with the dummy about yourself.

Many students may say being the ventriloquist is harder than being the dummy because it is up to the ventriloquist to specify discussion topics. Here are some topics from which the pairs can choose, but, of course, other topics made up by participants are encouraged.

- Why do *I* have to be the ventriloquist?
- Are you a real person?
- Help me choose my clothing for today.

- Why do I bother keeping you?
- (Choose an inner conflict about feeling or beliefs.)
- Do you like your face?
- It's time for your bath!
- How should I act when I'm with (mom, dad, teacher, brother, sister, friend, etc.)?
- Should I sit with the new kid at lunch?
- Should I grow up to be an artist or a scientist?
- I want to go to a party, but no dummies are allowed. How do you feel about me leaving you for a while?

When you start to combine dummy-ventriloquist pairs, topic possibilities expand.

- Two dummies talk about their owners.
- Humans want to swap dummies, but how do the dummies feel about that?
- What do you learn in dummy school?
- One dummy can ask the other dummy's ventriloquist a question.

Roles: Ventriloquists and dummies. Maybe a dummy school instructor.

Variations: This one is complicated enough already!

Classroom Variations: This is a good first-week-of-school role play. See the Classroom Role Plays and Creative Activities chapter.

Psychology: This role play focuses on feelings about being manipulated and on being the manipulator. It is about understanding how it feels to not be in control of your words or body, or to say something you personally don't believe or want to say. If having a hand placed on your shoulder or back feels uncomfortable, that means it's working because many people feel uncomfortable when someone else is in control of them. Also there is the flip side; it is about understanding how it feels to be manipulating or controlling another person.

Cautions: The primary caution is to be polite, respectful, and not silly. Remember, if the ventriloquist acts disrespectfully with the dummy, what do you think will happen when they switch roles? Be sure to remind them of this.

Notes: It is important to discuss this role play afterward. Focus on feelings of being controlled and manipulated, and being in control and doing the manipulating. Bring in the issue of verbal bullying and how it applies here.

Your notes:

Human Robot

Description: Divide the group in half, making sure your two best role players are in different groups, as they will need to play the difficult robot roles. Each group has received a factory-fresh robot which has not been taught anything except basic getting-around (motor) and language skills. The goal of each group is to teach the robot how to do something, for example, brushing your teeth or doing your chore such as washing the dishes. The players of both groups choose the same thing to teach, then each group goes to a corner to teach their robot the skill. Come back, and each group shows what it's robot has learned. Make sure the robot only does what it has been taught. You should try to listen and provide feedback as the robots are being taught.

Roles: Robots and teachers of robots.

Variations: Choose a task where each robot is taught something different but must interact with the other robot to perform it, such as throwing and catching a ball or ballroom dancing.

Classroom Variations: Use as-is, but you may want to have the creation relevant to something being taught.

Psychology: The robot must learn to analyze every action in order to see if it is something that was taught, making it a lesson in real-time logical (and perhaps literal) thinking. The other players learn about consequences, as they get to see the results of their teaching or lack thereof. The kids learn by having to create something from scratch, together.

Cautions: The person playing the robot needs to have a lot of self-control and needs to be reminded how to act, only knowing what it has been taught.

Notes: This role play can be very similar to the Summer Science Experiment if a robot is what the kids created, so it would be best to separate these two role plays in time by a month or more. You may need to point out the differences between the two role plays if a child says they already did that.

Your notes:

Cave People

Description: This is a three subgroup role play. Homo sapiens, playing anthropologists, go back in time to where Neanderthals and Cro-Magnon cave people both live, and the groups interact. The Neanderthals are the most primitive, limited to grunts, pantomime, and the occasional single word. Maybe not quite reflecting ancient history, Cro-Magnon are more similar to the Neanderthals than the Homo sapiens but can use short phrases of basic ideas.

Roles: Two Neanderthals (your more mature players), two Cro-Magnon, and the rest play Homo sapiens anthropologists (or student anthropologists if no one wants to play an adult).

Variations: With a group of less than six members, drop one of the cave person subgroups.

Classroom Variations: Use this role play as a reinforcer when learning about human evolution.

Psychology: This is analogous to the child being able to play someone very or somewhat younger. One might suggest these three subgroups represent child, adolescent, and adult. Some children will be able to identify with and expand upon the "cave person" within us all.

Cautions: Be sure to keep the cave people, particularly the Neanderthals, within their limits.

Notes: Have the two sets of cave people set up their homes which should be close to each other to encourage interaction. The Neanderthals should be encouraged to adapt their body language to the situation, that is, to move around stooped over, while the Cro-Magnon players should be encouraged to move around more like, but not quite up to the level, of Homo sapiens. Allow the Homo sapiens to decide how they go back in time. Focus the role play on communications between and among the three groups. Share a meal.

Your notes:

Who Took the Strawberries?

Description: Based on your knowledge of each participant, his or her personalities, preferences, and underlying needs, you create the roles for each person. The initial scenario as described soon is a starting point, but let the players take the role play where they may. Allow some give and take when describing the roles. The roles are advisory and meant to give you a starting point. While this role play is designed mostly to just have fun, a role may involve a challenge for a member you believe is ready.

Roles and Scenarios: You may suggest personality aspects or ask what personality goes with the name.

- Chief Inspector Popsicle (first name, Double)
- Inspector Rainbow Sherbet
- Resort Employee Cookie Crumble
- Guest Banana Split
- Guest Hot Fudge Sunday (middle name Fudge)
- Guest Dr. Cheesecake (hidden first name Strawberry)
- Guest Lemon Meringue
- Guest Salty Caramel

Make a big deal of naming each person. Scenario: While vacationing at a winter resort, someone took the strawberries! Who took the strawberries? Privately, you tell Dr. Cheesecake that s/he did it and to admit to the first name near the end. Choose a more self-controlled role player for Dr. Cheesecake.

Left just to that, an experienced group can take the role play in all sorts of directions and may enjoy the opportunities to be creative.

Variations: Create the roles, maybe have in mind who gets which role, but let the players decide who gets which role, and they can change a role too if it fits within the scenario you provide. Or even just describe the scenario and have members come up with roles for each other (not for themselves!), which a mature group might enjoy.

Psychology: The players will like that you spent the time trying to come up with good roles for each, and usually they will show their appreciation by giving the role play a little extra effort.

Cautions: Be ready to give up on the whole thing if the kids don't like it.

Notes: None.

Your notes:

Blind, Deaf, Mute

Description: Each player chooses one of the blind, deaf, or mute disabilities. Helping each other, they must find their way out of a dense jungle.

Roles: People who are blind, deaf, or mute, ages as chosen by participants.

Variations: None of significance because of lessons being taught.

Classroom Variations: When learning about disabilities, have one child wear a blindfold and have a few put their dominant arm in their pocket or in a sling. If you can get a wheelchair, that works well. Have the kids spend about an hour with their disabilities, and then have them switch with others. Be sure to discuss afterward and emphasize new respect for those with disabilities.

Psychology: Experiencing a disability is a valuable experience, as is helping another with a disability or communicating with a disability. Discussing afterward helps make this a more realistic lesson.

Cautions: You should explain what mute is. It is important after the role play to talk a few minutes about people with these disabilities, how difficult it can be, but also how special they are, such as increasing of other senses. Ask the kids to describe how they felt with their disabilities.

Notes: Players must be aware of and remember each other's disabilities. Clearly, the blind person needs the most help, but only s/he may hear a threat coming because his or her other senses are heightened. The jungle must be dense to make it important to help others with every step they make. Imagine debris and root-filled uneven ground with a dense canopy, making it hard to see your way.

Your notes:

A House in the Woods

Description: Kids go for a walk in the forest, get lost, then come upon an old house where they meet a couple of eccentric adults.

In this role play, you can create roles specific to the preferences and/or needs of your players, or you can use some classic personalities provided below. By later in the year, you may have some idea of personality areas where each of your group members can gain growth or self-understanding, and chosen or assigned roles can help. For example, the hyper kid could be given the personality of someone calm and peaceful, while the mellow kid can be given the opportunity to try on a little hyperness.

Roles: Kids and two adults. Here are a set of eight personalities, mostly grouped into pairs, representing some iconic characters.

The Kids

- Bad (Early) Teen (Age Thirteen): Your bad is like playing tricks or pranks on others, like putting salt in someone's cool-aid, rearrange someone's clothing, or small lies such as saying you will study with your friend but you go to a movie instead. Come up with ones of your own, where you don't actually hurt someone or their feelings.
- Bad (Early) Teen (Age Thirteen) Wannabe: You want to be like the Bad Teen, but you are not sure how to act. You really want to learn how to be a "bad teen," but you feel wrong or guilty for trying to be bad. You want to be a part of the group. You are sensitive emotionally, so you tend to get upset about small things, but you try not to show it.
- Hyperactive: You want to be always busy, doing something. You talk a little fast, you move a little fast too. You wave your arms about when you talk. You even think fast. You want to get things done. Sometimes you start to say something and forget what it was in the middle.
- Mellow: You are calm and peaceful. You are all about being relaxed, mellow. You want people to just slow down, take their time, and enjoy the doing part and not just the end result.
- Thinker: You like to think before you do. You like to make plans and let others act them out. You know lots of facts (during the role play you can make up facts and say them like you read them in a book). You act like you know what you are doing and that your ideas are good.
- Do-er: You tend to act before thinking. You don't know many facts, but you have a natural feel for what is needed in a situation, and you can only describe it to others in broken words.

The Adults

The two adults are a couple who have been married for many (at least thirty) years. Both people have strange and unusual personalities. This could be a same sex couple, which creates all sorts of interesting interactions in children this age (especially if you have a child in the group with two moms or dads).

- One: You like to throw your mystic stones to tell the future. Even for small stuff. You are naturally friendly and loyal, kind of like a dog. You like everyone. You are more of a feeler than a thinker.
- Two: You would rather think and talk about something, and you think the mystic stones are silly. You are more reserved, and people need to earn your friendship, kind of like a cat. You are more of a thinker than a feeler.

If strong feelings come up, if at all appropriate, end with a group hug, lasting a little longer than usual, and a discussion.

Variations: As stated earlier, these are suggestive personalities. If you want to go beyond just having fun, you can replace all or some with personalities representing what you and your group think could provide a self-understanding and growth experience. Remind them they are here to grow and that if you feel a little uncomfortable, it may be because the role means something to you.

Psychology: With a focus on personalities and open-ended directions in which the action could move, this role play is more psychologically oriented than most others. It focuses on self- and social-understanding, allowing members to take roles that represent some part of their personality that could be focused upon for personal growth.

Cautions: Prepare the group by telling them that this role play can be a complex one that may sometimes challenge their feelings, and remind them that if they feel uncomfortable, it means there is something for them to understand about themselves.

Notes: A concluding group discussion is a must for this psychologically focused role play.

Your notes:

Chapter 6

Micro Role Plays

Over the years, the author has been challenged with situations where kids could not focus for long, so he developed some short-duration scenarios that last just a few minutes and that use one to four participants while the remainder watch as an audience. Micro role plays are also useful to fill extra time at the end of the group, they can be used as "warm up games" for a lethargic group, and in the classroom, they can serve the purpose of class members becoming comfortable in self-expression.

Create a semicircle of chairs facing a "stage," with two or three extra chairs ready to use if the scenario calls for it.

These short scenarios can be presented in two ways. One is for you to have them printed on a master sheet where you choose the scenario and then read it out loud. The other is to cut them up into one scenario per slip of paper, fold them, and place them in an envelope from which the player blindly chooses one and reads it out loud. Usually require them to do the one they choose, or else you will quickly run out of scenarios. Get them to agree to this beforehand, and also that if they choose one, they must do it and cannot skip. But any player can skip a turn by not choosing a slip from the envelope. If you use the master list, remember to check off the ones you use, because you may not return to the list for several weeks.

Below are listed seventy-six micro role plays, including some spooky ones for Halloween at the end. Several could lead into full blown role plays if the players want, and many can be repeated by other members if it catches their fancy. Hopefully, you will have as much fun as the author in making up more scenarios.

MICRO ROLE PLAYS

Tell us a story about the Evil Frosted Cupcake and its plans to take over the world.

Make up a story about a child who has no legs.

Make up a story about a child who has one leg.

Make up a story about a child who has three legs.

Giant slugs are taking over the earth. Make up a plan to stop them.

You are the leader of the giant slugs who are trying to take over the earth. What is your plan?

Make up a story about how a computer got feelings.

Fit everyone into the smallest space you can.

Your mouse has no tail. How did that happen?

Make us believe you won a prize.

Why is your hair laughing at you?

You have a third eye in the middle of your forehead. What is it for? Teach us how to use *our* third eye.

Show us Sponge Bob Square Pants at a clothing store.

You look like you are getting smaller. Why?

You look like you are getting bigger. Why?

Tell us a story about a hungry child. Do not use the word "the."

You wake up in the kitchen with your mouth full of string beans. Your family is looking at you. What happens next?

Your parents are sending you to summer math school! What will you say to them?

You get to school on a very cold day. When you take off your hat, you have no hair! What could you say or do to make this a good thing?

You get on an airplane for a tropical vacation, but you get off the plane in Alaska. What happens next?

Choose a partner. You are a fish who gets caught. Talk the fisher-person into throwing you back.

You know what people near you are feeling and thinking. Go up to some (or all) people and tell them what they are feeling and thinking.

Choose someone to be a school teacher who is very depressed and wants to quit. Give a pep talk to keep on teaching.

You are a student who is depressed because you can't remember what you learn. Choose someone to be your school teacher, and have a conversation.

Pretend you are visiting your parents at the old folks home.

Pretend your parents are visiting you at the brain damage hospital.

Your computer responds to voices. When you tell it to do your homework, it says no. Convince it to do what you tell it to do.

Here is a glass of Ugly Purple Glop. Be a salesperson at a store and try to get us to buy it.

You are two people on a Saturday afternoon. One of you wants to go see a movie. The other you wants to go home and sleep. Let's hear your two selves talk about this.

Your special research has shown that the next time it rains, the rain will have frogs. When you warn people, they don't believe you, so you make up a story that would make people believe. What is that story?

You are fishing off the end of the dock when something big pulls on your line. You try for a while, but then you must ask the homeless woman or man next to you for help.

Four people are in the deep forest, where the trail splits into two trails. Three must take the very steep uphill branch and one must take the very dark downhill path.

Four of you wake up in a narrow two-person tent. No one can get the zipper open.

You are your teacher and have to meet with the parents of your real self, to talk about how you are doing.

You are your mom or dad and have to meet with your child's teacher about how your child is doing.

You are very afraid of frogs. Your three best friends are trapped in a cage in the middle of Frog Island. Can you rescue them? What do you say to give yourself courage?

You have a really cool mom. You bring home some of your friends, to plan a party for next Saturday. But your mom does not act cool. Instead, she treats you like a little kid.

Your new tree house holds only three people. Three of your friends show up to play in it.

There is a new student in your class who is *very* serious about *everything* and never laughs or plays. During recess, three other students decide to get to know him or her.

There is a new student in your class who jokes about everything and can never be serious. During recess, three other students decide to talk with him or her about it.

It is your first day in junior high. Unfortunately, your imaginary friend insists on going with you. Your imaginary friend keeps talking to you, trying to get your attention.

You are on a field trip with your class to the science museum, and to show off you say you know all about the volcanoes exhibit. So the teacher asks you to give the lesson.

Your parents dropped you and your older sibling off at the giant new toy store in the big city. They said they would pick you up in one hour. They are now a half hour late. What do you do?

You wake up in a different house. The parents and the other two children think everything is normal and that you belong. What happens next?

In the forest, you find a mother and father crying. When you ask what's wrong, they say they cannot find their daughter or son, but that you look just like him or her. What happens next?

Make up a story about a boy/girl and his or her pet dragon.

Make up a story about why all the invisible people decide to become visible.

Make up a story about why a group of children decide to become invisible.

Make up a story about why the children *had* to take over the United States when no one else could.

Make up a story about snow that came up out of the ground instead of falling from the sky.

You get a letter from your future self warning you about something. What does the letter say?

You are on a roller-coaster when it gets stuck right at the top of the biggest rise. The adult who got put next to you is very frightened. Even though you are scared too, you have to comfort the adult.

You are in a hall of mirrors at an amusement park. Step in front of a mirror that makes you look really tall, and have a conversation with yourself in the mirror.

You are in a hall of mirrors at an amusement park. Step in front of a mirror that makes you look really short, and have a conversation with yourself in the mirror.

You are the mother or father of a family who gets lost in the jungle in a rain storm.

You are the oldest sister or brother of a family who gets lost in the jungle in a rain storm.

You have two heads with different personalities. Have a discussion about what to do after school.

You are afraid of clowns. You go to the circus to challenge your fear. What happens?

You are with three friends. Everyone except you wants to trespass into a playground which is closed for the weekend.

Everyone else in the world becomes frozen like statues. What do you do?

Suddenly you are in the body of your mom's friend, sitting with her on the couch. Ask her how she disciplines her child. Play *both* roles, your mom and her friend.

There is something different with the way you look. People try not to laugh when they see you. Everyone else knows what is different except you, but they don't feel right telling you. Figure out what is different and tell us.

It is your turn to make breakfast for us all, and we get to watch! But when you crack an egg, a chicken comes out. When you try to cook the bacon or sausage, a pig appears instead. When you put bread in the toaster, wheat comes out. And when you try to pour a glass of milk. . . .

You are a vampire who just became a vegetarian. Have an argument with yourself about what to eat.

You are a witch or warlock, but the people under your control are too simple to know they are not in control of themselves. Try to get them to understand they are in your power.

You wake up the day after Halloween with a stomach ache. You look in the mirror and see your skin has turned an ugly shade of green. Choose three people to have breakfast with, then come down the stairs for breakfast.

The day after Halloween, you have become what your costume was yesterday. Choose people for your teacher, plus one or two friends. Start the scenario when you enter the classroom.

SPOOKY MICRO ROLE PLAYS FOR HALLOWEEN

You eat a large piece of Halloween candy, but it starts moving around inside you.

You're at the doctor, lying on the table. You fall asleep and wake up to the doctor cutting you open. She is saying, "Where did I put that baby?"

When you ask the teacher to help you, she starts spinning like a top and throws bits of flesh all over you. You can't seem to move.

You wake up while your mom is dressing you . . . on a serving tray. She has your stomach open and is filling you with turkey stuffing.

You look in a hand mirror and see you are getting very old, and bits of your body start to fall off.

An invisible force grabs and starts to shake you. When you cry out for help, it puts its hand over your mouth.

You reach for a piece of candy from the big candy bowl, but when you put a piece into your mouth, it turns into an eyeball. Each piece you try turns into something gross; a finger, half a child's human liver, rotting maggot flesh, and a whole foot.

An invisible force is removing all your face parts and putting them back in all the wrong places.

For the whole group: Halloween candy is across the room, but for each step you sink deeper into the floor.

Chapter 7

Creative Activities

Creative activities make good companions to role plays, they can provide "filler" time at the end of the group, and they can help in developing role play ideas at the beginning of the group.

None of the included creative activities are new or unique. All of them, in one form or another, have been around for many years. You may recognize several of them under different names.

Below are listed twenty-seven creative activities which have been used. Over a third of these creative activities were taken or adapted from a book published originally in 1909 but revised in 1937.[1]

As with role plays, some creative activities are "just for fun," but several have underlying psychological and/or educational meanings or goals. Some are very short, some longer, and some can use whatever time you want to fill. Some can lead to role play ideas too.

As with role plays, creative activities are listed from simple to complex, from early in the group process to later.

Mirror

Description: Pair up members, with a threesome if you have an odd number of participants and spread them out in the room. First, each pair chooses a leader, then the leader makes slow and controlled movements, including facial gestures, while the other member follows. Switch roles and redo.

Classroom Variations: This would be a good ice-breaker in a class just starting up in September or just beginning to use role playing.

Psychology: Having power over another's movements is empowering for children in this age range, and being able to give up this power and to follow can be a bonding experience.

Notes: You will need to remind that slow movements can be mirrored but not so well with fast ones. Rotate the threesome more frequently so all have turns leading.

Your Notes:

Circle Story

Description: Sit on chairs in a circle. One person begins a story with about one to three sentences, leaving off in the middle of a sentence, then the next person continues the story, and this continues around the circle as many times as you want. Usually, you start the first few stories until members catch on. For example, "On a warm summer day, I was sitting in the middle of a lake in a row boat, when suddenly . . . . " Or, "I woke up to find I was floating twenty feet above the grass in a park. I looked down, and I saw myself playing with my friends. The me on the ground looked up and . . . . "

One alternate is to have each member say just between one and three words, but usually the result is not as robust as with the traditional method. But this can be fun after doing it the regular way a few times.

Another alternative is to target the circle story to certain areas or topics. A good one to use is circle story in a refrigerator. If you use this and don't get any "vertical integration," when it's your turn, add it, so that, for example, veggies interact with things in the freezer compartment.

Classroom Variations: This might be a fun way to start the day, but just go around once or twice. Perhaps focus the topic on something relevant. If working on a play, do a circle story limited to items and activities found in the theater, on the stage or in the play.

Psychology: Members learn to think fast on their feet, to give up on a planned idea because it conflicts with what was just created, and they learn to better appreciate others' strange thought processes. Also, the group spirit is strengthened by this shared creation.

Notes: This is a very popular creative activity that can be used several times in the course of a year.

When the story is passed on, be sure the new person's words continue the story, even if it changes everything. Some people will not want to give up what they planned to say and may ignore what was just said.

Your Notes:

Finger Squeeze

Description: Sit in a tight circle, with knees almost touching. Tell members
   to hold together the index and middle finger of their left hand and reach it
   toward the group member to their left. With their right hand, squeeze the
   two fingers given to them from the person on their right, as hard as they
   can. Say, "squeeze with the right hand," then usually you will need to add,
   "the other right hand."

Emphasize having each person remind the member to their right to "squeeze
   tighter" whenever the pressure lessens and to relax the shoulder and elbow
   because "it's all in the hand."

After about a minute, tell members to open their right hands just enough to let
   the person next to you slip his or her fingers out. Then ask members to gently blow into their cupped right hand to cool down the skin and muscles.
   Then, emphasizing the word "slow," to tell members to "open your hand,
   as slow as you can."

Classroom Variations: This would be fun in grades three and four, perhaps
   five, as a way to bond early in the year, but it has little educational content
   beyond learning the difference between left and right. Older children might
   enjoy the biological explanation of how this works.

Psychology: The strangeness of the feeling seems to have a strong effect on
   children. At this age range, they are beginning to understand what their
   bodies actually can do, and it is a strange but good thing to them. Group
   bonding is enhanced with this shared strange feeling.

Notes: The first time you do this, there will be some confusion, and some will
   open their hand as soon as they let go of the person to their right. Remind
   them it only works if you open your hand slowly. Also, you will need to
   remind most members to just tighten the hand and to leave the shoulder
   and elbow relaxed.

Members will ask to do this all year long.

Your Notes:

Poor Pussy

Description: The children sit in a circle on the floor or in chairs, with one member in the middle who goes to each person and pats them on the head, saying three times, "poor pussy." While saying "poor pussy," the person can exaggerate their expression or voice. If the person being petted laughs, they trade places, with the laugher becoming the person in the middle.

Psychology: Learning not to laugh when encouraged to do so is a lesson in self-control.

Caution: Some religions say the soul is in the head and touching the head may not be okay. If there is a sensitive member, have the group touch a shoulder instead of the head.

Notes: Some members will enjoy "loosing" to get a turn in the middle.

Your Notes:

Beast, Bird, or Fish

Description: Sit on the floor in a circle. Take a piece of letter-sized scrap paper and ball it up. Underhand toss the ball to someone in the circle and say one of the three; beast, bird, or fish. The person to whom you tossed the paper ball is to say out loud the name of an animal in the target group you named. Then that person tosses the paper ball to someone else, saying one of the three words (beast, bird, fish). It is best to make it go fast. The same animal cannot be used twice.

Classroom Variations: This game would be a good reinforcement of something recently learned. After teaching about biology, history, geography, anything with lists of things, limit the responses to one of the categories, such as U.S. capital cities. Break up the class into groups of at least four members so everyone can play.

Psychology: This teaches fast thinking, and if/when members favor their friends with their ball toss, it gives you an opportunity to reinforce that the group is the focus, and choosing different people to toss toward is a way to show respect for the group.

Notes: Rarely does a group want to play this a second time, so get the most out of it when you use it. This makes a good companion with Buzz.

Your Notes:

Buzz

Description: Sit in a circle and go around, counting up from 1. For every number that either has a 7 in it, or is a multiple of 7, say "Buzz" instead. You could have members who get something wrong sit out, or just move along without consequences to failure.

Classroom Variations: Use as is, maybe changing the target number around. For younger children, it can be good practice for learning the times tables.

Psychology: Little, but it reinforces math knowledge.

Notes: Usually, members don't want to do this one a second time. Primarily, it is a short duration time filler. If you have a group of seven, then change the target number, or else the same person will be buzzing over and over. This makes a good companion with the creative activity Beast, Bird, or Fish.

Your Notes:

Hands in the Middle

Description: Members stand in a tight circle with shoulders touching. They reach in with their arms and hands, and each hand grabs one other hand. The group then tries to untangle themselves into one large circle without letting go of each other. Some will end up facing into the circle, while others will end with facing out.

To begin as a simple creative activity, start with just three or four group members. Then add members as decided by the group. If they have trouble with more people, ask if they want to stop and return to this again later in the year when they have a little more experience. This activity can be both simple and complex.

Classroom Variations: Similar to Finger Squeeze, this could be a fun way to bond your class early in the year, but with grade four and above.

Psychology: Working together is the key, but also it's interesting if a leader asserts him or herself.

Notes: Tell members to loosely hold the other hand, to let the hand rotate as you move about.

Your Notes:

Blind Draw

Description: Give a letter-sized blank piece of paper and a pencil to each child while sitting around a table. Ask them to hold the pencil and place the point in the middle of the paper. Then have them close their eyes and ask them to draw something. First try geometric shapes (try a circle first), then try a house, but quickly move on to faces and other more interesting objects such as trees, a skateboard, or a swing. Then ask them what they want to draw. Remind them they are on the honor system, that if they peek, they are denying themselves the fun of making strange shapes.

Classroom Variations: This can be used as described. It can be used as a game to help focus an overactive class. If appropriate, add a lesson on Picasso, since many faces will look similar.

Psychology: The kids really seem to enjoy this. Perhaps it is an opportunity to make mistakes, not only on purpose but also because no one can be expected to draw an object more complicated than a simple geometric shape with their eyes closed. No one is expected to make a bilaterally symmetrical face.

Notes: A few kids have done remarkably well with circles, triangles, and squares.

Your Notes:

How Long Is a Minute?

Description: Have the members sit so they can't see a clock. Using a watch with a second indicator, or using a "count up" stopwatch so it does not sound a tone when time is up, first set a time frame for the members. Begin with twenty seconds. Say "ready, set, go," then time your twenty seconds. When each member thinks it's time, they quietly raise their hand until all have done so. Then try thirty seconds, then longer as chosen by the group.

You try to note how early or late members are, in order to give them feedback for the next round. This can be difficult, trying to watch the time while hands are going up, but with practice and peripheral vision, it can be done. Usually, point out the number of seconds the first hand was early, then the person(s) who were within a second or two, then the number of seconds for the last raised hand, and the others can judge themselves in comparison.

Classroom Variations: Use as is. It can help calm and focus the class while teaching how to keep time without a clock.

Psychology: Mastery is an element in terms of tracking time internally.

Notes: It is amazing how well this works. Overactive groups calm down immediately, and it is a game kids ask for again.

Your Notes:

Ruler Drop

Description: Take a one foot ruler and hold it with index finger and thumb by the top edge so it hangs down twelve inches. Tell the member that when you release the ruler, s/he is to grab it between his or her index finger and thumb before it passes by. Have the member hold his or her index finger and thumb about three to six inches below the bottom of the ruler. After the first drop, adjust the distance between the bottom of the ruler and the member's fingers to make it easier or harder. If you have enough rulers, pair up members and have them do it with each other.

Classroom Variations: Use during a lesson that involves coordination or reflexes.

Psychology: Fast reflexes are encouraged by this activity.

Notes: A meter or yard stick is too long for this activity to work.

Your Notes:

Whiteboard Relay

Description: Begin by using one colored easy-erase whiteboard marker, making one line or curve near the bottom of the board (some kids won't be able to reach too far up). Taking turns, each person adds one line or curve, building up a picture of something. After the first one, add additional colors for effect. After the first creation, name what is chosen to draw before you start to draw it.

Classroom Variations: This could have some relevance to creating a picture of something related to a recent lesson, where you would say beforehand what the end product will be.

Psychology: This can provide a group bonding experience.

Notes: The first time you do this, there is a chance the final product will be abstract art. Emphasize trying to create something, even if you don't say what it is beforehand.

Your Notes:

Who Laughs First?

Description: Everyone stands or sits in a circle and looks into each other's eyes. The person who laughs first can either take a step backward out of the circle until just one is left, or just redo with everyone. After each round, discuss what one can do with feeling and thought (but not with muscles) to suppress the laugh. Repeat to test new strategies.

Alternately (or after practicing the above), have a friendly competition. Pair up and stare at your partner. Winners face each other until only one remains.

Classroom Variations: This makes a good group bonding experience early in the school year. Divide the class into groups of six or eight.

Psychology: While learning strategies of self-control, group bonding is enhanced.

Notes: The members should look directly into the eyes of others, use only blank faces, and use no muscles, expressions, or "scrunching" the face together to suppress or cause a laugh. Consider any sort of smile a laugh, including the attempt to hold it in (i.e., compressing lips).

Either before you start or when you see it happen, discuss playing fair. Make sure people don't use tricks to not see, such as crossing the eyes, not looking directly into others' eyes, fast blinking, and similar avoidance methods.

Discussion can include feelings of discomfort when looking into another's eyes, what type of self-control does it take to do this, and whether learning self-control here can carry over to other classroom behaviors.

Your Notes:

Who, What, When, Where, Why, and How

Description: Sit around a table and give each member a letter size piece of paper and a pencil. Start by writing Who, What, When, Where, Why, and How down the side of the paper, leaving space between each. Beside Who, write a person's or character's name. Fold it over so you can't see "Who," and pass the paper on to the next person who then writes an action next to "What," folds it over and passes it on. Continue until How is filled in, then each member opens his or her paper and reads what was written.

Classroom Variations: Combine this with a specific lesson related to people, and limit what the students write down to the topic of the lesson. For example, when learning about types of jobs, the Who would be the job title.

Psychology: Group bonding is shared with this usually funny game.

Notes: Don't worry about spelling. The time this creative activity takes is partially dependent on writing skill of the members.

Your Notes:

Hide the Thimble

Description: Ask group members to close their eyes while you hide any small object in the room, so that at least some of it shows when just walking around. That is, don't make it so you have to stand on tippy toes or get on the floor or lift something to see some of it. Members walk around to find the object. When a member finds the object, s/he is to not say anything or act differently but is to continue to pretend to look for a minute so, then go sit down. This is to give every member a chance to find the object. Repeat, giving each member a chance to hide the thimble.

Classroom Variations: While perhaps too active in some classrooms, the lesson of not ruining the fun for others can be a valuable one. Possibly, make it a daily activity with one person per day hiding the thimble, and being chosen to hide the object could be some sort of reward for exceptional behavior.

Psychology: The primary lesson is delaying gratification by not indicating when you found the object. They learn it is important to let everyone enjoy the feeling of finding the object. Self-control is required to not ruin one's fun with peeking while the object is being hidden.

Notes: Emphasize the rule about the object being visible while standing.

Your Notes:

Word Association

Description: While sitting in a circle, you say one word, and each member then says the word that first comes to mind when they heard the word just before them. Keep it going fast; if someone can't think of what to say, that person can skip that one turn.

Classroom Variations: This could make a fun start to the day and perhaps give you an idea of what is in your students' thoughts.

Psychology: Free association in psychology taps the subconscious, although this may not always be the case for children in this age range.

Notes: This is a method to help loosen up an overly controlled group or a group having difficulty coming up with a role play. You can take the words given and see if there are any common themes which then suggest a role play idea.

Also, sometimes it can give you an idea as to the psychology of the group on that day.

Your Notes:

Body Sculpture

Description: Each member takes a turn at being the artist. All other members are clay and have no will of their own. The floor is your platform. The artist begins by naming the sculpture s/he is about to create, then s/he, by a combination of verbal commands, modeling, and physical manipulation, creates said sculpture. Sculptures can have motion and sound if desired.

If the artist places someone in an uncomfortable position, that piece of clay can say "memory," then relax in near-position ready to resume when the artist is almost finished creating.

Psychology: The power of the artist is absolute. Being clay makes it okay to be manipulated, and the kids enjoy this too. Also, there is an element of working together to create something, particularly if the parts must interact.

Notes: You may need to make a reminder that all but the artist are clay, and since clay has no opinion or will, it means nothing if, for example, you are placed in contact with the other gender.

It is a good idea for the leader to go first in order to give the players a better idea of what is in mind. Start by creating a sculpture that has most of the elements allowed. A simple one is a clock; two people for the hands, one player is for striking gongs at the top of the hour, and the remaining members can make up the circle of the clock. Also, there is the human body while digesting food; head, lungs, stomach, and a small person can play the food. With enough members, add an arm to put the food into the mouth. The kids enjoy the gross factor, and everyone is making different motions while close to each other, so it also involves give and take and an increased awareness of those around you.

Your Notes:

Three Questions

Description: Choose a member to go first, and have that person step out of the room. Then the rest of the members make up three yes-no questions. The person reenters the room and answers the first question *before it is asked*. Then the question is revealed. Do this for the other two questions, then repeat for all group members.

Psychology: "False" embarrassment, at this age, can be fun.

Notes: Some kids may have trouble catching on to the types of questions best asked. Once you give a few examples, the members can add on others. Offer a few examples. Do you wear your underwear on the outside? Do you have a belly button? Is your name (choose name of other gender)? Have you ever cheated on a test? Do you have a child of your own? Does 1+1=2? If you wear polka dot underwear, say No. If you have baby kittens frolicking in your underwear, say Yes. Are you your self? Did you shave your beard this morning? Do you want to go back to preschool? Did you grow up from the ground, like a tree?

Try to avoid questions that may embarrass, such as, do you suck your thumb?

You will find that saying yes is much more fun than answering no.

Your Notes:

Find the Ring

Description: Sit on chairs in a circle with enough room for one person who stands in the middle. The sitting members pass, from hand to hand, a small object (small enough to be hidden in a child's closed hand) in front of their bodies, that is, not behind their backs. A member can hold onto the object and pretend to pass it on. After about thirty seconds, stop passing the object. The person in the middle tries to guess who has the object.

Psychology: This teaches visual focus and enhances group bonding.

Notes: Someone may be selfish and keep the object for himself or herself more than once. Remind that person about selfishness and ask if it helps or hurts the group.

Your Notes:

Observation

Description: Have the members gather around a table. Then place about ten (hand sized or smaller) objects on a tray or the table. You can bring objects or just use anything in the room. If you do not use a tray, place objects close enough together so that they are about the same dimensions as a dinner tray. Ask the members to close their eyes (preferred, as it teaches self-control) or turn away from the table. Move one object a small amount, maybe just rotating it, or perhaps switch two similar objects. Ask members to open their eyes, look for the change, but don't say anything until everyone has had a chance to identify what is different. Repeat, possibly adding objects, moving more than one object, or letting members move objects.

Classroom Variations: You can use this as is, or maybe use objects related to a recent lesson, for example, different types of leaves, and have the kids name the leaves that were moved.

Psychology: A general sense of mastery may result if one is successful at this activity. Patience is taught by having to wait until everyone is done before saying what has changed.

Notes: If a member points out the change right away, remind him or her that others want to feel the same enjoyment of discovery and to wait until others have had a chance.

Your Notes:

Picture Show

Description: Take some letter-sized paper and cut it in half lengthwise so you have two long strips. Sit around a table, and hand out a paper strip and a pencil with an eraser. Have each person draw a simple picture, using the top three or four inches and taking no more than three minutes. They write what the picture is on the very bottom of the paper strip, then they fold just the bottom of the paper so as to hide what they wrote. Pass the paper to the next person who looks at the picture and writes what they think the picture is, also on the bottom of the strip, just above where the paper was folded over to hide the bottom most line. Then fold the paper again to hide what was just written. This continues around the table until you get your own picture back. Remind members not to unfold the paper yet. One by one, each member holds up the picture s/he drew in order to remind members what it is, then s/he unfolds the paper, one line at a time, and reads out loud what each member thought it is, until s/he gets to the last line which is what it really is.

Psychology: Children in this age range are beginning to become aware of their idiosyncratic thinking, and they enjoy seeing others get what they drew either right or wrong.

Notes: This is a very popular creative activity. Note, however, that it does take time; at least a half an hour, possibly forty minutes, for a group of eight. The smaller the group, the less time it will take. You do have opportunity to chat with members between passing on the picture strips.

Your Notes:

Who Am I?

Description: Take something similar to a 5 × 7 index card and make two corner holes for a string to place around the members necks. On each card, near the top, write the name of a prominent person, a cartoon character, or anyone all members know (e.g., the school principal). See appendix I for some examples. Players walk around and make comments to, and ask questions of, other members until they are able to guess who they are.

The key is to comment or ask questions that do not make obvious who the person is. Give clues that help just a little. So for Red Riding Hood, you would not go up and say, "what a pretty red riding hood you have." Instead, one person might say, "you seem to like red a lot," and other might ask "what's in the basket you are carrying," while a third may ask if they are visiting a relative. Only if the member has difficulty guessing who they are should be clues become more and more obvious.

Classroom Variations: Use as is, in relation to a history lesson. For example, use names of presidents, thus making the kids use their knowledge about specific presidents. Or the names could be cities or even parts of the human body or a tree.

Psychology: The art of asking a leading question, without it being too leading, is a valuable skill which this age range is just beginning to learn.

Notes: Between each round, you will collect the cards, cross off the old name, and write a new one from your master list, then replace the cards around their necks.

This is a good activity on a day when the role players cannot seem to choose a role play.

Your Notes:

Optical Illusions

Description: Simply share a set of optical illusions with the group, usually starting with the more simple ones and advancing to the more complex ones. There are plenty of images which work when printed, but if you have an Internet connection, illusions-in-motion create additional possibilities.

Classroom Variations: This is really fun and can be a lead-in to discuss how people see things and how the brain works.

Psychology: This serves to open the mind in a way to support creativity.

Notes: It is beyond the scope of this book to include the optical illusions which have been used over the years. However, there are many sources on the Internet, and there are books available filled with optical illusions. Two excellent sources which are advertisement free at this time are http://www. eyetricks.com/illusions.htm and http://www.michaelbach.de/ot/.

Your Notes:

Touch Memory

Description: Have members sit around a table, and give them a piece of paper
and a pencil. Ask them to close their eyes. Then you place some objects,
which you had kept hidden, on the table. Start with three objects. With
eyes closed, the kids handle the objects, after which you remove them from
view. Then have them write down the names of as many objects as they
can remember and identify.

Classroom Variations: Use this in conjunction with a lesson, using objects
pertinent to the lesson.

Psychology: Memory is what is primarily taught.

Notes: Don't worry about spelling.

Your Notes:

Crambo

Description: Cut letter-sized paper across, into three or four inch strips. Each member gets three slips of paper. On one slip of paper, they write a question, on another, they write a noun, and on the third, they write a verb. Make three mixed piles, one each of questions, nouns, and verbs. Then each member draws one slip from each pile. Verbally, they must answer the question, using the noun and verb they drew. Decide as a group what to do if you select what you wrote. Some will be okay with it, others will want to redraw.

Classroom Variations: Use as is, mostly for younger children when learning about the differences between nouns and verbs.

Psychology: Not much, except perhaps a lesson that one can be creative within bounds.

Notes: Emphasize spelling means nothing in role play. We're all about the ideas.

Your Notes:

Taxi Driver

Description: Download or recreate appendix H (see appendices for the link).
Sit at a table, and hand out appendix H along with a pencil. Tell members
that the lines in the upper left corner represent the taxi driver garage, where
you start. You then call out numbers (i.e., houses) one at a time, not repeating any. Members are to draw a line from the garage to the first house,
then the second, and so on, but they cannot cross any line already drawn.
A good starting sequence begins with 11–6–20–16–19–1–10–9–13, and
continues with your choices.

Classroom Variations: Use as is with the entire class. Plan to do it twice (print
front and back), so kids have a chance to apply their learning.

Psychology: It's all about learning to plan ahead and learning strategies from
experience.

Notes: Consider the first time a trial, so print on both sides of the paper. Bring
two sheets of paper per member so you can do it four times. There is a best
strategy, which you (but only a few kids) may be able to figure out after
the first couple of times.

Your Notes:

Touch Recognition

Description: Have members stand in a circle, with one member in the middle. Try to have them pull their hair back away from their faces (or have another member silently hold the hair back). Remove any eyeglasses. Blindfold the middle person, turn him or her around so s/he does not know who s/he is facing, gently lead that person up to a group member, take the middle person's wrists, and gently guide them toward the outside member's face. The middle person is to gently touch the face, and only the face, and identify who that person is.

Psychology: There is an intimacy to touching another's face, and this reinforces group bonding.

Notes: Because of the intimacy, this game should be done after the group has bonded. It is easy to identify someone by his or her hair, which is why it's important to keep that away from the face. Silence is important, both in voice and body movement, so touch can be the only way to identify. If you have a short person, have that person stand on a book or two or something appropriate to bring that person to a similar height as other members. If there is a tall person, others could crouch or stand on books.

Your Notes:

Hands Up! Hands Down!

Description: Divide into two equal sized groups, and each group chooses a
   captain. Each group sits at a table facing each other across the table. One
   group passes a quarter from hand to hand under the table. When the captain
   of the other group says "Hands Up!" they place their hands on top of the
   table, palms up, and with fingers closed in order to hide the quarter. The
   opposing team can look for as long as they want. Then the captain who
   just said hands up says "Hands Down!" Simultaneously, the members slam
   their hands, with the palm open and down, onto the table, making lots of
   noise (just with their hands, no shouting) to disguise the sound of the coin.
   The captain consults his or her group and chooses a hand it is *not* under,
   and that person removes the hand. Only the captain can ask the opposing
   team to turn over a hand; members should talk with each other, but the
   captain verbalizes the group decision. The most empty hands uncovered
   before the coin is found wins. Choose new captains or new groups if members desire and repeat.

Classroom Variations: If you want to teach how to work together in a group,
   this could be used with a class party. Three or four members per group
   works best.

Psychology: Selfishness is addressed in the passing, or not passing, of the
   coin. Group cohesion is addressed by the need to simultaneously slam
   down your hands. And patience is taught by only the captain being able to
   turn over opponents' hands.

Notes: The key is to slam your hands down simultaneously, otherwise the
   opponents will hear under which hand the coin resides. After the first
   round, when they figure this out, you could give each group a couple of
   minutes to practice.

This is a good game for the last group meeting where you may have a party.

Your Notes:

NOTE

1. Bancroft, Jessie H. *Games* (New York: Macmillan Company, 1937).

Chapter 8

Guided Imagery with Relaxation

Guided imagery is a technique used to "rehearse" behaviors before they are acted. Athletes use this to review and focus before competition. Those making a presentation can use this to rehearse what they might say. This technique has been adapted to role play so that the leader guides the imagery, rather than the athlete or presenter themselves. It is like a "role play of the mind."

For the kid's sake, this has been renamed to "Fantasy Trip" which accurately reflects the adaptation of this technique. Ask each member to lay on his or her back or side (on your back is better for the relaxation part) on the floor with sufficient room between so that no one can touch another. Have them close their eyes and not talk, so they can all focus on the leader's voice. You will have to remind some of the kids that the only voice should be yours.

Begin with a relaxation game (don't call it an exercise which makes it sound like school), where you have them tighten then relax specific muscle groups. Traditionally, this starts at the feet and works its way up the body, but personal experience suggests starting at the top helps the kids better focus. Have them "tighten and release" their hands, followed by arms, face, torso, butt, thighs, then feet. Be sure to mention not to tighten too tightly; just to the point before it starts to hurt. At each muscle group, with a relaxed voice, name the body area, then say "tighten," pause a second or two, then say "release." After going through these body areas, ask them to slowly tighten their whole body, then quickly release.

Then it is time for a fantasy trip, most of which have psychological meaning. Fantasy trips can also lead to role play ideas. For example, in "What's in the Box," each player finds something in his or her box, and you can ask how to make up a role play, collectively, with each of the things they found.

Some of these are written as "ready to read," while some are outlines. For all of them, feel free to use your own words, since the underlying theme is the key. And if you feel comfortable, go ahead and make up your own, even if they have no underlying meaning, because sometimes role play is to just have fun!

What's in the Box?

It is a warm summer day. You are in a rowboat on a lake, enjoying the feeling of sun on you, when a gentle whirlpool draws you to middle of the lake. You take a big breath and hold it as you get sucked down into the water by the whirlpool, but then you see a dome under the lake with an opening at the top where the whirlpool leaves you. You pry open the air lock, close the outside door which makes the water drain away and lets you take a giant breath of air, then you open the inside door where you find a staircase. You walk down and down to the bottom where there are three doors from which to choose, and each door has one word on it. You choose a door, and inside is a room with a box in the middle, on the floor. You can't quite tell how large the box is until you walk up to it. You then open the box.

You: Discuss what is in your box and what word was on the door.

Underlying Meaning: Their choice of word and what they find in their box might reflect subconscious desires but more likely will reflect what is on their mind that day.

In Search of the Golden Thing

It is a summer morning, you are dressed for hot day. You can feel the cool wind on your arm, and it makes you want to move and explore.

You notice a boulder the size of a medium dog, and you say "g'mornin." It says, "Where is the Golden Thing?" Huh? You look behind the tree, and tree asks, "Where is the Golden Thing?" You look in a shed, and the shed asks, "Where is the Golden Thing?" You look under a fist size rock which asks, "Where is the Golden Thing?"

You heard there is a circus in town, so you go there. You visit the merry-go-round and notice a golden ring every time you go around. Finally you grab it and ask, "Are you the Golden Thing?" It says, "Dear human, I am a ring, not at Thing." You put the golden ring on your head, and it grows larger until it falls down over your body and causes you to be transported to a dark small room with big chest. You step into the chest and close the lid, then step out into middle ring of three-ring circus where you are expected to perform! You tame the lion, ride the wild horse, leap over a car with clowns, and suddenly you become one of the clowns crammed inside car. Other clowns leave by the doors, but you find a trapdoor, which leads into a dark and mysterious land where you wander around looking for golden stuff.

A storm roles in. Thunder says, "Where is the Golden Thing?" and sends a bolt of lightning which you grab out of the sky. The lightning bolt takes you up into the clouds where you meet wise whales. You jump onto the back of a whale and ride it for a while before asking, "Where is the Golden Thing?" It says, "Look inside." Huh, inside what? It's hard to understand the logic of whales. You see a building glinting gold in the sun, and the whale drops you off. You go inside and find it empty! You go back out and ask again, "Inside what?" It says, "Yes." It's hard to understand the logic of whales.

So you ask to look inside the whale. It starts to hum, you go inside, into the belly of the beast, but nothing golden can be seen, so you crawl out smelling of half-digested fish.

The whale looks you in the eye with a dinner plate sized eye, and you see your reflection. You stare deeply, and you grow smaller and smaller, until you get small enough to go into yourself. You see some blood, some guts, some dark, and some light. You know all about blood and guts already, having just been inside the whale, so you turn toward the dark and see images of you being sad and of you being happy. You don't like looking at the sad, so you turn away to the light, but all you see is emptiness, just light.

You find some courage and enter the dark again, moving deeper inside yourself, inside your mind, and you feel both sad and happy. Deep inside yourself, you find another trap door. It smells odd but you enter anyway, deeper and deeper inside yourself. You feel uncomfortable looking at your dark side, but you chose this path and are determined to finish what you started.

Finally, you reach a very small area, the deepest corner of your mind. There is another trap door, which, of course, you enter and find the most inside, the deepest, part of yourself. And, it is golden! *You* are the Golden Thing.

You: Ask what they liked best about the fantasy trip and what made them feel uncomfortable.

Underlying Meaning: This teaches the importance of understanding what is inside your mind, your personality. It also reinforces looking at the uncomfortable in order to better understand yourself and to grow as a person.

Mastery: The Alien Test

You all fall unconscious. Your minds have been captured by alien invaders, leaving your unconscious bodies behind. Your bodies look like they are sleeping, except your face twitches with what is happening inside your mind. Your mind is in an alien space ship, in a virtual reality environment. It's like being in a video game, it feels real to you, but it is only in your mind, without your body.

The aliens want to know how humans will react to being taken care of. Do humans like to do things themselves, or do they like to have things done for them?

They give you a mastery test. They want to test how good you are at doing absolutely nothing. You are given one eager servant, a servant who *wants* to take care of you, who *must* take care of *every* need and desire you have. The servant feels that s/he has failed if you have to lift even one finger. First it is time to eat, and the servant spoons food into your mouth, then takes hold of your chin to help you chew, then carefully rubs your throat to help you swallow. Then there is your art painting, and you must tell your servant exactly what color to put where. Your exercise is a foot race, but you just lay back and watch your servant run for you. Finally it's time to sleep, and your servant changes you into your sleeping clothes, turns you over, and scratches your itches (where ever they might be) all night long. After one week of this, you are offered to switch roles and become the servant for one week.

You say: Everyone sit up so we can talk before we end this fantasy trip. How did it feel having *everything* done for you by the servant? Did you feel the same after a week? At the end, did *you* choose being servant for a week? Why? Do you think the alien's test was a good test?

Now, I would like to hear each of you tell the group your end of the story. Pick up after you have been taken care of for a week and you were offered the chance to switch roles and be the servant for a week. What happens next?

Underlying Meaning: This is about independence (self-mastery). How the players end the story might reflect what they are concerned about within themselves.

Mastery: Look at Yourself

During breakfast on a school day, your mom whispers a word in your ear, adding that you will need that word soon. When she says the word, you have a brief feeling of fear, then you feel a little bit powerful, then like yourself again, and then you forget all about it.

So you climb into the family car and drive yourself to school, thinking nothing about how hard it is to see over the steering wheel or reach the gas and brake pedals. You stop for gas, the attendant takes your credit card and thinks all is normal. When you get to school, you see the parking lot is full, but then you notice a car exactly like yours, but you can see through it, like it's only half there. You drive into that space, and your car merges with the other so it becomes solid. You wonder what that was all about, but you don't want to be late for class.

When you get to the classroom, someone is already in your seat, and that person looks just like you. Your double is talking with your friends. You jump up and down and shout, but no one sees or hears you. Everyone in the class believes that person is you! But then your double works on your art project and is not doing it the way you planned, so you concentrate really hard and try to get into the mind of your double. You want to control him or her, not just for the art project, but also because you are afraid your double may say or do something really silly and people won't like you anymore.

You concentrate really hard again, trying to control your double's mind. At first, your double's hand won't do what you think it to do, but you get better control with practice. Then you concentrate harder and hear your double's thoughts and its plans for what to do at recess. It's not even focusing on the task at hand, so you try to give it a thought about how to make the project better. At first, it does not work, but then you remember the word your mom whispered to you at breakfast, so you say that word out loud, and suddenly you switch roles with your double. You are sitting with your classmates working on the project.

You: Ask what happens next? What can you say to your friends to explain your double's behavior? Discuss how it feels to watch yourself in action and talk and to have only some control of what you say and do. How were the thoughts of you and your double different? What was the word your mom whispered to you?

Underlying Meaning: This illustrates how you can use thoughts to understand and control yourself and your feelings.

The Ship Who Sang

(Thanks to Ann McCaffrey)

You go to sleep paralyzed and wake up as the controlling brain of a space ship. You see through cameras, and you are able to move on your own with your engines. No longer tied to a wheel chair, you decide to tour the solar system. You visit the floating whales of Jupiter. You check out cold Neptune, then head out to interstellar space. You end up near a black hole and decide to go through it. You exit through a white hole into an alternate universe. You take a tour of the alternate universe and find the alternate earth. Everything looks the same, but as you watch, you see animals walking or swimming backward and over time you see trees growing younger. You realize that time is running backward in this strange universe, and then you think the last thing you want is to grow younger. So you head back through a white hole, then the black hole, to get home.

You: Discuss what being a ship brain was like and how it felt. Discuss what it might be like to be totally paralyzed and be set free, with your body being a space ship and never again to have a human body.

Underlying Meaning: This is about self-control and about how choices can change the direction of your life.

Self-Confidence

You have been chosen to make a presentation to adults on "how to help your child to feel self-confidence." You have no idea how, so you take a walk, end up in a meadow next to a pond with geese and a fire pit. You start a fire and put the pan on it, then you fall asleep and have a dream where the geese grab you and fly away with you. They toss you back and forth, you have no control, until one misses, and you fall into the frying pan. You jump around without a plan until you accidentally jump out of the frying pan and into the fire.

There you find others like you trying to spread a silvery blanket over the fire so you all don't burn up. The heat of the fire keeps making the silver blanket flop around until you try using magic. You draw a symbol in the air, say a few words, then the silver blanket becomes rigid. Remember the symbol and words you just said. You help the others climb onto the blanket, then they pull you up last. It turns out you really made a magic carpet, and you take control to fly away, but the heat from the fire fools you, and you crash land in the pond. You don't know how to swim, but you've seen others do it, so you teach yourself to swim, then you save all the others.

You: Discuss being in control of your body and how helping others helps you feel more confidence.

Underlying Meaning: This is about being self-confident.

Tide Pool Thoughts

At the ocean, looking into a tide pool. Put your hands in and share thoughts and feelings with each other. Now touch something and share thoughts and feelings with it. Sponge (I'm thirsty), piranha (I'm hungry and angry), anemone (squeeze me, I'm lonely), puffer fish (bubbles, no troubles!). Ask them to swim around and touch two other things. Ask members to remember what they touched and it's thoughts and feelings.

You: Discuss the idea of sharing thoughts with others, if it feels like an invasion or bonding experience, what it would be like to be able to hear others' thoughts.

Underlying Meaning: This considers the growing need for privacy, beginning at this age. It also deals with the related concept of what is "me" versus "not-me."

Evolution

Begin by saying you are a single cell, then advance through evolutionary stages (slime, plant, fish, centipede, frog, dinosaur, bird, leopard, ape, human). End with a future focus, saying that maybe humans evolve into balls of energy without bodies.

You: Ask which form they preferred to be and what would they do in their final form.

Underlying Meaning: There is not a lot of underlying meaning, but ending with not having a body can create some fertile topics of discussion.

Where to Live?

While flying without aid, pass through various environments where people can live, such as desert, rain forest, mountain, caves, under the ocean, by the lake or river, and so on. Be creative in your choices of environments, as this is a fantasy. Describe each environment as you fly through. Have fun describing some actions going on.

You: Ask which place would they would rather live in and why.

Underlying Meaning: While mainly just an adventure, the environment in which a child might want to live may reflect basic personality predispositions.

Pig on a Platter

When you wake up, you are a whole roasted pig, on a platter, at a dinner party. Children are gathered around you, talking about who gets what part of you to eat. You hear one ask what is the best part of you to eat, so you say, "Maybe you should have my leg. I'm very tasty there, and I've been exercising it too. It's nice and firm." So off goes your leg, and your thoughts goes with it, into the mouth, then to the stomach and then to the brain where you, as the roasted pig, can hear the thoughts of the child who ate you. You think this is not so bad because it is a child much like yourself.

The child then goes to the park to play, but right away the child is eaten by a huge rubber ball as big as a car. So now you as a pig are inside of the child who ate you, and the giant rubber ball that ate the child. You can hear all the thoughts of the child who ate you and the rubber ball's thoughts too. But who is in control? Can the ball or pig control the child?

Suddenly you are the rubber ball, with a child inside, and a roasted pig inside the child. You find yourself on a path that divides. You the ball wants to go one way, while the child inside wants to go the other way. The pig only wants to be eaten so does not care which way to bounce. When you the ball start to move, you the child concentrate really hard, trying to get control of the giant ball. After some back-and-forth, you are the stronger mind and you make the ball go the way you want. Of course, after all this work, you had to eat the pig inside you because you were very hungry.

You: What do you do when you have conflicting thoughts, when part of you wants to do one thing but another part of you wants something else?

Underlying Meaning: This is about dealing with conflicting desires and about self-control as well.

Appendices

Appendices

Note: These Appendices are reduced-size, black and white, representations. Ready-to-use (full size and color) appendix items can be downloaded from the publisher's website (https://rowman.com/ISBN/9781475830385/Teaching-Social-Skills-Through-Role-Play-Second-Edition/features/RolePlayAppendices.pdf). However, unles you have PDF editing software, you will need to re-create the application (appendix A).

Appendix A: This is discussed in chapter 2 under Recruiting. This is one example of the information and sign up sheet for the role play group. It has been tweaked over the years to emphasize the need for self-control and trying new things. In this example, the start and due dates, meeting day and time, leader name and contact information, need to be replaced with your information.

Appendix B, C, D, E, and F: These appendices are discussed in chapter 3 under Five Presentation Items and are to be used in the first two or three group sessions. Respect (appendix B) is the global value, under which the other six values (appendix C) can go. The three steps to role play are illustrated in appendix D, and the two keys for role play are presented in appendix E. appendix F considers the concept of moving forward in terms of getting the members to grow socially and emotionally.

Appendix G: This goes with the Quest role play described in chapter 5 and is necessary for it. You will need just one copy when you do this activity.

Appendix H: This one goes with the Taxi Driver creative activity in chapter 7 and is necessary for it. You will want to make as many copies of this as you have group members. Copy them front and back so your group can do it twice if they want to.

Appendix I: This goes with the Who Am I? creative activity discussed in chapter 7. You will want just one copy of this to mark up as you progress through this creative activity. Feel free to add and delete items as people go in and out of child awareness over time.

The appendices are available in color online at https://rowman.com/ISBN/9781475830385/ Teaching-Social-Skills-through-Role-Play-Second-Edition. The content will be on the features tab.

!!!ROLE PLAY!!!

FOR 3rd YEAR LOWER ELEMENTARY

Creative Activities Teaching Social Skills and Self Understanding

Wednesdays, 2:45 - 4:15. Starts September 21st - Thru May

(HOW I RUN THE GROUP) *READ THE BOOK*! (ALL THE ROLE PLAYS I USE)

AVAILABLE IN THE LIBRARY & FOR SALE IN FMES STORE

Application Deadline: SEPTEMBER 14th

FREE! Regular Attendance Expected. No more than 8 participants. FREE!

Pre-Requisites: Participants MUST be able to use self-control and have a positive attitude.

Acting skills helpful but not necessary. Willing to try new, sometimes hard things. No roughhousing. Humor recommended!

Read Testimonials from FMES Parents and Professionals on the Reverse Page!

Who Makes a Good Match for Role Playing? [Parents, please help child understand this.]
It is important that the child understand the goal of role play is self-understanding or learning about yourself, and that self-understanding occasionally might involve trying something new or taking a role that feels a little uncomfortable or difficult. That is how one grows and learns about one's self. Role play creates opportunities which can be tried out in a safe and non-failure environment. The group comes first. A child who has difficulty going along with the group majority would not be a good match for role play.

I encourage the members towards self-control, and they lead the group as much as possible. I challenge them to work together to solve problems and to try new and different roles, even if it makes them feel a little uncomfortable for a few moments. I allow no put-downs.

Examples of Role Plays
Adventures in Aftercare: 2 students are aftercare workers and step outside the room while the rest of the group create typical scenarios such as a student won't share, said something mean, etc.
Restaurant: Waiters and chef get things wrong.
Self-Empowerment: Parents forget how to take care of themselves; child must help parent.
Robot science experiment: Create a robot, teach it to have feelings and interact with others.
Aliens!: Peaceful first contact; aliens land in a park. How do you communicate?
Micro Role Plays (short, under 3 minute, role plays): Family, school or other scenarios such as family dinner, want to stay up later, care for your sister/brother, sibling disagreement, home alone, sent to office at school, public school student visit, emergency room visit, convince a fisherperson to throw you back, etc.

Who am I? I am Dr. Christopher Glenn, Research Director (Retired) at FMES. This is my 33rd year of role play at FMES. My background is in counseling and psychology.

I am usually only at the school once a week, on Wednesdays for role play. I would ask you to communicate directly with me, via phone or email, rather than leaving notes for me at school. I can be reached at xxx-xxx-xxxx or by email at cglenn@xxxxxxxxx.com.

Please complete the attached form and leave it at the receptionist desk in the entryway.

From Parents (pertinent to role play):
Role play is my child's favorite activity of the week. I love how it builds her confidence without her even realizing it, but it also has helped her work out problems at home and with friends. What she's learning about group work now she will carry with her into college and in any career she chooses. **(Allison McCormick, parent, FMES)**

My daughter's imagination, creativity, and cooperation skills have been greatly enhanced through her participation in Dr. Glenn's Role Play classes. She has had a wonderful time and doesn't even realize that she's learning. Bravo! **(Elizabeth Rouffy, parent, FMES)**

My daughter has raved about it all through the year and wishes she could continue taking part! She even brings some of the role play 'games/scenarios' home and makes the whole family play along and experience it. That tells me that these sessions have had quite an impact on her. **(Sheela Preuitt, parent, FMES)**

From Professionals (pertinent to the book):
Through extensive research, and grounded in everyday classroom practice, Christopher Glenn, Ph.D. the author of this book explores important issues surrounding role-playing within a Montessori curriculum and environment. The book presents children's views on, and responses to their role-play environment, alongside examples of good classroom practice. The author presents the child's perspective on play in schools throughout, and argues firmly against a formal, inflexible learning environment for young children. Dr. Glenn presents a work integrating the work of Maria Montessori into an environment of play, creative activities and guided Imagery. This book will be fascinating to all students and teachers in the field of education and in early childhood studies. Researchers and course leaders will also find this book a source and guide for role-playing within any educational environment. **(Therese Gutting, administrator, Franciscan Montessori Earth School/St. Francis Academy, Portland, Oregon)**

I am delighted to be able to recommend Role Plays and Creative Activities: Teaching Social Skills and Self-Understanding. Every day I am contacted by parents of gifted children who are having trouble fitting in with their age-mates or coming to terms with themselves as 'outside the norm.' Although it is designed for neurotypical children, I believe a program such as the one described would be a perfect intervention for gifted children, who often have significant emotional and social needs due to their unusual learning styles. A role play group such as the one described in the book could help them work out how to get along in a world that sometimes feels alien, because few others see the world the way they do. As an educator, I also appreciate the tips for using these activities in a whole-class environment as well as in a dedicated extracurricular program. I look forward to being able to share this book with our local Gifted Youth Coordinators to enhance their work with our young members. **(Lessa J. Scherrer, National Gifted Youth Coordinator, American Mensa, Ltd.)**

Christopher Glenn has written a very useful and engaging book on the use of role playing with children. He thoughtfully and wisely informs the reader with explicit detail about how best to conduct role playing activities (as well as other creative pedagogical designs), attending to the concrete details of how to set up such activities, how to explain their nature and processes to children, and how to debrief them for the greatest educational advantage. The book contains a large number of specific role play designs, with the author's notes about when in the course of a school year they might be used (early, later) and at what age levels different activities might best work. Advice also is provided to the educator wishing to develop her/his unique activities.

This book is a fount of wisdom, gained from the author's vast experience as an educator. It will be very useful to school teachers, social workers, and counselors working with children and to parents seeking home activities that might buttress children's personal, interpersonal, and civil learning at school. **(Mark Chesler, coauthor, Role-Playing Methods in the Classroom)**

<u>IF YOU PLAN TO ATTEND GIRLS BASKETBALL IN JANUARY, PLEASE DO NOT SIGN UP.</u>

Times for girls basketball and role play overlap. I do not allow kids to leave early because it disrupts the psychology of the group, and the debrief at the end is important.
****

Role Play Application
(Deadline: SEPTEMBER 14th)

I would like my child to participate in Dr. Chris Glenn's Role Play group, every Wednesday after school from 2:45 to 4:15. If I need to cancel a week, I will try to let Chris know, by email or phone. **I will talk with Dr. Chris if I decide to quit the group.**

Parent Name:_____

Student Name:_____

Phone:_____

Parent Email:_____

How often do you check your email?

_____ Two or more times a day

_____ Once a day

_____ At least every couple of days (i.e., okay for contact if not urgent)

_____ Less often than the above (i.e., not a good way to contact me)

*****

<u>Student Part</u> (Parent, help child understand this if necessary)
My mom or dad has talked with me about role play, that it is usually fun but sometimes challenging, and that sometimes I have to go along with the group. I would like to participate in Dr. Chris' Role Play group, every Wednesday after school from 2:45 to 4:15. I hope to come almost every week. If I decide to quit role play, I will talk with Dr. Chris about it.

Student Signature:_____

Respect:
√Role Play Group
√Each Other
√Your Self

1. **Respect**
2. **Patience**
3. **Forgiveness**
4. **Flexibility**
5. **Understanding**
6. **Communication**
7. **I-CAG-WIW**

3 – STEPS For Role Play

1. Choose Topic
2. List Roles
3. Choose Roles

ROLE PLAY
Keys To Make It Work:

Feel Your Character's Feelings

Would My Character Say or Do That?

Progress
Or
Regress?

ProGress=Move Forward

ReGress=Move Backward

Role Play: Quest

Scenario:
[Younger ages:] We're going on a Quest for either a way to end world hunger or for treasure. Which one?

[Older ages:] We're going on a Quest for...something. Let's first decide what our quest is for. It could be something physical like treasure or your kidnapped parents, or it could be something else like a way to end world hunger or gain self-confidence.

There are [number of group members] obstacles you must work through:
1. Valley of Fog
2. Wind Mountain
3. Wall of Fire (20 feet wide)
4. Flood Plane
5. Crack in the Earth (10 feet wide)
6. Tornado Alley
7. Quick Sand
8. Earthquake Country

For each obstacle:
[Younger ages:]
1. Choose a group leader.
2. Do it once to find out what you need to do it right.
3. Do it again after gathering supplies.

[Older ages:]
1. Choose a group leader.
2. Brainstorm and discuss options and ideas.
3. Make your plan.
4. Gather supplies.
5. Do It.

Rules:
You <u>must</u> work as <u>one</u> group. No one is allowed to work on their own.
You cannot go around any obstacle. You must pass through each of them.
No mechanical devices (no motors or engines).
You can carry more than you normally can, but nothing absurd like a helicopter.
If you are injured, you stay that way for the rest of the role play.
If you die, you are out of the rest of the role play. But you can watch.

|||||

7	11	3	13	17	4	10
16	9	1	6	18	2	19
14	5	12	8	20	15	21

Easter Bunny

Harry Potter

Snoopy

Princess Lea

Darth Vader

Albert Einstein

Rudolf Reindeer

Scooby-Doo

[School Principal]

Mini Mouse

Queen of England

Sponge Bob Square Pants

[School Vice-Principal]

Fred Flintstone

Santa Claus

Gandalf

Charlie Brown

Tinkerbelle

3CPO

Bugs Bunny

R2D2

Mickey Mouse

Barney

Tarzan

Cinderella

Snow White

Pocahontas

Sherlock Holmes

Sleeping Beauty

Rapunzel

Robin Hood

Peter Pan

Pinocchio

Wizard of Oz

King Arthur

Little Red Riding Hood

Dumbo

Alice in Wonderland

Hercules

Mary Poppins

About the Author

Dr. Christopher Glenn experienced his first role as an infant in 1952 and progressed through various child roles until adolescence where he experienced some complications through which necessary creative skills were developed in order to advance into the brief role of valedictorian (1970). Dr. Glenn spent the next decade in the role of college student, assuming undergraduate (1974), masters (1975), and doctorate (1980) characters. Finishing college in the roles of both child and psychologist, he promptly assumed the professional role of education, survey, and market researcher, while maintaining a relationship with a unique Montessori school serving children through eighth grade. In 1984, he created and assumed the role of Role Play Guy with the nickname of Dr. Chris, where he transformed his adolescent survival-necessitated creativity into a proactive force of imagination, inspiration, and invention. Simultaneously, he assumed the role of research director at the school, conducting twelve studies over twelve years. Dr. Chris has assumed the role of Role Play Guy about 950 times over the past thirty-three years.

While Dr. Chris has earned his most recent role of retiree, he still maintains his website (http://www.glennresearch.com) and continues to develop his role as Role Play Guy, occasionally creating new role plays and adjusting group processes. He enjoys the leisure roles of hiker, sitter-in-nature, photographer, and gardener, and is the victim of modern home entertainment.

www.ingramcontent.com/pod-product-compliance
Lightning Source LLC
Chambersburg PA
CBHW030651270326
41929CB00007B/318